# Malamud's Fiction

## A Discourse of Authenticity and Acceptance

# Malamud's Fiction

## A Discourse of Authenticity and Acceptance

S.S. GILL

Prestige
an international publishing house

*Published by*
**Prestige Books**
3/28, East Patel Nagar
New Delhi 110 008
Ph. 9818755529
email: prestigebooks@gmail.com
website: asiabookclub.com



Printed at Chaman Offset Press, New Delhi 110 002

# Contents

## Acknowledgements

I express my deep sense of gratitude to Dr. Shelley Walia whose sagacious guidance, sustained encouragement and loving support enabled me to complete this project. I cannot close these prefatory remarks without acknowledging my gratitude to Senior Academic Associate, the Librarian and Staff-Assistants of American Studies Research Centre, Hyderabad who helped me during my visits, and provided me study grant twice that proved to be of great help. I am grateful to Dr. Deepak Manmohan Singh, Dr. Gurpreet Kaur and Jaiteg Gill for their constant support and encouragement. I sincerely thank Professor R.K. Dhawan of Delhi University for suggestions made to bring out the project in the published form. Finally I put on record my appreciation for Prestige Books for bringing out the book most expeditiously and elegantly.

**SUKHJINDER SINGH GILL**

# Introduction: Struggle for Recognition

In the second half of the twentieth century man's mind has registered spectacular triumphs over nature. Notwithstanding his triumphs, he feels uneasy and bewildered. While his power over matter grows, he feels powerless in his individual life and in society. All of Bernard Malamud's fiction is an attempt to understand and order the chaos of experience in the twentieth century. His fiction reveals the vulnerability of the individual in the mass capitalist societies resulting in his helplessness and devaluation and the loss of his humanity and values. Therefore, it becomes imperative for the individual that he should be open to 'other' and accept the responsibilities that follow such openness. Although we find Darwinian struggle for survival and recognition in his fiction, the criterion of fitness for survival ultimately is not sheer physical strength but moral vigour. The main struggle for recognition is invariably to gain a better understanding of others and to find authenticity and acceptance by them.

Writing his first novel, *The Natural*, as early as 1952, Malamud could not escape the spirit of the twentieth century. The protagonist of his fiction, an 'isolato' of the modern era, strives for meaning and individuality in a perverse world. Projecting and bringing into perspective the modern experience of meaninglessness and emptiness, Malamud creates his protagonist as experiencing the inability to participate in all relationships and experiences. As a result, instead of self-affirmation, there is a sense of despair and non-being. However, Malamud does not bring down the curtain on the protagonist in the throes of despair. A strong sense of optimism permeates his fiction converting the apparent agony and suffering into triumph. Malamud's protagonists stand up against the demoralizing forces not by ignoring them but resolutely facing up to them and finding strength to live morally in spite of them. Nihilistic forces reduce man to insignificance but he can prove his worth by maintaining his dignity in spite of all afflictions and seeking value and order in his life. "There are unseen victories all around us," states Malamud, "it's a matter of plucking them down,"[1] by striving hard and with courage.

Bernard Malamud himself affirms his stance as an artist: "My work, all of it is an idea of dedication to the human. That's basic to every book. If you don't respect man, you cannot respect my work: I'm in defence of the human."[2] Time and again Malamud has complained that American fiction "is loaded with sickness, homosexuality, fragmented man. . . . We are underselling man."[3] Conscious of the fact that much of current fiction is "underselling man," Malamud defines the purpose of a writer thus: "to keep civilization from destroying itself."[4] He firmly believes: "Art, in essence, celebrates life and gives us our measure."[5]

Thus, as per his commitment, Malamud portrays, "against the unquestionable dwarfing forces of modern society, the honest often successful struggle of the individual striving to define himself as a man within a narrow range of active possibilities."[6] He believes that man is basically good, however lowly the circumstances of life may have made him. Each can redeem himself because each has the capacity to do so through suffering. In an interview in 1961, Malamud said, "A bad reading of my work would indicate that I'm writing about losers. One of my most important themes is a man's hidden strength. I'm very much interested in the resources of the spirit, the strength people don't know they have until they are confronted with a crisis."[7]

However, this does not mean that Malamud distorts reality nor is his universe Utopian. His feet firmly planted in this world, he speculates on man's possibilities. Evincing a deep sense of awareness of the devaluation of man, Malamud clearly defined his note of affirmation and acceptance in 1958 when he was awarded the national book award for *The Magic Barrel*:

> I am quite tired of the colossally deceitful devaluation of man in this day; for whatever explanation: that life is cheap amid a prevalence of wars; or because we are drugged by totalitarian successes into a sneaking belief in their dehumanizing processes; or tricked

> beyond self-respect by the values of the creators of our own thing-ridden society . . . or because, having invented the means of extinction, man values himself less for it and lives in daily dread that he will in a fit of passion, or pique or absentmindedness, achieve his end. Whatever the reason, his fall from grace in his eyes is betrayed in the words he has invented to describe himself as he is now: fragmented, abbreviated, other-directed, organizational, antonymous man, a victim in the words that are used to describe him, of a kind of syndechdohic irony, the part for the whole. The devaluation exists because he accepts it without protest.[8]

Deeply involved with the situation of the contemporary man, Malamud's fiction explores man's struggle for recognition and further evaluates his moral responses to experience of authenticity and acceptance through a meaningful committed relationship with others. As his fiction shows, Malamud refuses to engage in the devaluation of man. His compassionate vision and the transforming power of his warmth invest the little, inept, fumbling figures who constantly appear in his fiction with dignity as well as pathos. As David Boroff puts it, "essentially, Malamud has redeemed failure, a valuable service in our hard-lunging success culture."[9] In each of his story, he affirms his faith in the ability of man to realize and recognize himself even in the face of deprivation and disaster.

Malamud in his fiction projects something of the paradoxical condition of contemporary man in America. The hero who emerges brings with him both the helplessness of man in the face of the forces of dehumanization, mechanization and conformity and the hopefulness, as futile as it may seem, of triumphing over these very forces. The hero is caught in a now familiar existential dilemma: man victimized by a world he never made and yet yearning for transcendent power and a privately satisfying sense of self. Ihab Hassan's rebel-victim is Bernard Malamud's typical hero for he combines in one paradoxical figure both the victim hero and the self-asserting hero. Among Bernard Malamud's heroes, Frank Alpine and S. Levin are examples of this type. They are alienated from society, groaning under imaginary or real grievances. The victim and rebel are two guises under which 'the hero' appears, and after the identity of the victim and the victimizer is confused.

Malamud creates a hero, "who realizes the confusion and absurdity of modern [American] society but who, instead of rejecting the society, is determined to discover a truthful way of action in it."[10] Malamud's heroes strive for a fate good enough to fulfil a sense of a privately satisfying self. Their quest is personal but they must make it through the recognizable social world. They confront the oppressive forces that undermine their active quest for selfhood and authenticity. The confrontation between the hero (activist or victim) and the world, between an individual and the shaping forces in public life, is central to the fiction of Bernard Malamud.

The ultimate achievements of the Malamudian hero are ambiguous. In any event, a quest for recognition, a commitment to the imperatives of self, does not necessarily and inevitably bring productive results. However, what is laudable is their courage to try and forge a personal identity in the face of worldly schemes. The breakthrough they achieve, however negligible, is by a desperate act of will.

The surface story of Malamud's fiction is usually about a modern quest for a more prosperous life and the failure of such a quest. Beneath each story of defeated ambitions lies the theme of moral growth of the hero through his experiences. Malamud himself affirms that he chooses to, "go along the same paths in different worlds"[11] and though the locale differs in different novels, his moral vision remains consistent. The basic theme in each novel is derived "from one's sense of values, it's a vision of life, a feeling for people—real qualities in imaginary worlds."[12] Caught between materialistic and idealistic imperatives, the hero is made to realize his moral obligations. As Marcus Klein says, "Morality is simply the name of the discipline. . . . The story to be told, consequently, is of the hero who becomes heroic either by rising to acceptance of obligation or descending to it."[13]

Malamud's primary concern is with the hero's quest for a meaningful 'new life.' The theme is based on the experience of rebirth. Man falls but is given a chance to redeem himself by accepting his fate (for better or for worse) and within it transcending his weak self, to become an integrated self. The stress in the process to maturity falls on making the hero realize his humanity which is shrouded by egoism and expediency. In self-transcendence lies the protagonist's heroism.

Thus Malamud's basic theme is the "possibility of human salvation and identity through a consciously constructed personal ethics."[14] All Malamud's heroes have, at first, purely materialistic aspirations. All of them seek to break through their mediocre lives the limitations of their unfulfilled lives. Each envisions his future in terms of the American myth of wealth and fame. However, Malamud's theme of recognition and acceptance demands that the characters realize the illusory nature of their romantic preoccupations with a new life. Humanistic values rather than materialistic values must govern their lives if they seek authenticity. They must learn to discipline themselves and thus transcend their selfish desires, for such desires are self-destructive. It is through a painful process that the heroes are initiated into the reality of life. The process of initiation is both slow and painful but at the same time it is a comic experience. From selfish concerns, the hero must pass into a life of involvement and responsibility towards others. From egocentric concerns he must proceed to ego-denial. He is expected to make his own covenant with others based on love and compassion. It is through love and suffering for others that the hero can achieve self-transcendence and acceptance.

However, the self-realization is achieved in terms which are essentially Jewish. Like most of the contemporary writers, Malamud responds to the present experience by choosing subjects and locales that are apparently remote from that experience and yet very close to it through their inner quality. Irving Howe clarifies this aspect of Malamud's work, when he writes about the general character of the contemporary writing:

> Abroad, the past, or the few pockets of elemental type, many of our best writers have pursued exactly these strategies in order to suggest their attitudes toward contemporary experience. In *The Assis-*

> *tant*, Bernard Malamud has written a somber story about a Jewish family during the Depression years, yet it soon becomes clear that one of the impelling motives is a wish to recapture intensities of feeling we have apparently lost but take to be characteristic of an earlier decade.[15]

Malamud reaches the immediate experience through what is recognized as Jewish experience. One cannot escape noticing that Malamud's stories are distinctly Jewish in subject as well as technique, even when it is known that he means much more than what he says. Mark Goldman has explained the oblique perspective Malamud has adopted to the human condition:

> Malamud's rejection of social realism, however, allows him to capture the moment of crisis, when his characters transcend their suffering by remembering their common identity as Jews, and recognizing their human stake in the tragic predicament.[16]

It is clear from this that for Malamud the typical Jewish attitudes and sensibility have assumed the dimensions of an objective correlative for the archetypal human experience. However, since Malamud chooses the Jewish experience as a metaphor which is also a literal historical fact, he had to make it as authentic as possible. In view of the authenticity expected of him in depicting that indefinable, elusive Jewish experience, it was an advantage for Malamud to have been born Jew, for as an insider he is very likely to have a greater insight into it. With his remarkable artistry and inherited advantage of being a Jew, Malamud has successfully evoked that old world feeling in his tales. Discerning critics like Ihab Hassan have noticed the Jewish and the non-Jewish qualities of Malamud's work:

> Malamud's vision is preeminently moral, yet his form is sly. It owes something to wile of Yiddish folklore, the ambiguous irony of the Jewish joke. Pain twisted into humor twists humor back into pain. The starking of suffering, the laden weight of ignorance or poverty, the alienation of the Jew in a land of jostling Gentiles—all these become transmuted in luminous metaphors, a bittersweet irony of life, into something, finally, elusive.[17]

Bernard Malamud has been more successful in projecting viable and persuasive images of Jewish experience than the earlier

Jewish-American writers for the simple reason that his creative use of the core of Jewishness lifts it up from parochial concerns. He has extracted the seemingly undefinable Jewish experience from the particular of the Jewish social life. In other words, he has taken for creative use what is valuable in the Jewish experience, that is, the rich Jewish moral insight, the typical "ethic of hard work, integrity, acceptance of responsibility, forbearance in distress"[18] in the characteristic response to life, humour and pathos, in short, the Jewish sensibility.

Malamud depicts the Jew not in their religious ritualistic and conventional guises, but in their essentially characteristic response to the pain, the agony and the heartbreak of life. Malamud's Jews hardly share the religious, historical or sociological facts which generally identify the Jew as Jews. As Ruth B. Mandel recognizes:

> The Jew [in Malamud] is not used in a religious or ethic sense: he is symbol of modern man, a symbol of hopefulness, humility and isolation. Becoming a Jew always refers to a secular, personal, inner struggle; and the best Jews are those who become moral men while continuing to suffer because the nature of their moral code demands self-abnegation.[19]

Malamud's Jews share the racial ethic evolved by the Jews in their long historic suffering in exile. And, of course, exile and alienation are the basic conditioning factors of the Jewish sensibility. Malamud has discovered that this distinctly identifiable Jewish experience isolated and magnified reflects the general human experience. He has asserted more than once that he was mythologizing the Jewish experience, "the model not only of suffering and confinement but also of a very limited yet precious possibility of triumph in defeat, freedom in imprisonment."[20]

Malamud states: "Jewishness is important to me, but I don't consider myself only a Jewish writer. . . . I have interests beyond that and I feel I'm writing for all men."[21] Though his work is related to his Jewishness, Malamud asks for a literary rather than a narrowly, religious evaluation of his fiction; as a social realist, he takes as his domain the society that he has seen and known. Malamud is a humanist whose concerns are broadly moral and social; his artistic vision though rooted in the particularities of Jewish life, extends outwards to the common humanity shared by all men. Malamud states, "I write about the marginal Jew who manages to be influenced by the concepts of morality which incidentally are Jewish but not only Jewish."[22]

Thus Malamud's moral vision draws sustenance from the Jewish ethnicity and is within the Jewish tradition. Yet it is broadly humanistic rather than narrowly religious, for it concerns the need for love, charity and selflessness. As Philip Roth has aptly put it, Jews in Malamud's fiction "are Malamud's invention, a metaphor of sorts to stand for certain possibilities and promise."[23]

What we have, then, is a fiction whose flavour and frame of reference are often Jewish, but whose meaning extends through and beyond the confines of the Jewish experience. Malamud is able to merge the Jewish plight with the existential plight; a Jew's sense of rootlessness, persecution, exile and his quest for identity makes him an archetype of the fragmented modern man seeking purpose in life. The Jew becomes a metaphor for the oppressed's struggle to withstand the indignities of the modern world. Norman Podhoretz says, "To Malamud, the Jew is humanity seen under the twin aspects of suffering and moral aspiration. Therefore, any man who suffers greatly and who also longs to be better than he is, can be called a Jew."[24]

Malamud's Jews have roots in the *Schlemiel-schlimazal* figure of the Jewish folk traditions. He is "vulnerable, ineffectual in his efforts at self-advancement and self-preservation and emerged as the archetypal Jew, especially in his capacity of potential victim."[25] Malamud's earlier heroes like Frank Alpine, S. Levin and Yakov Bok, especially fit the role of the *Schlemiel* character. Victimized and self-victimizing, they seem to fulfil their destiny by suffering and their main qualities are humiliation, passivity and poverty. Their fate is pitiable but hardly tragic. Their experiences are simultaneously desperate and comic. Yet, their reactions to their plight elevates them to a position of dignity; they find sustenance in their never failing hope and their innocence.

Each of Malamud's novels, from *The Natural* to *God's Grace*, is indubitably the work of a dreamer who has taken upon himself the task of affirmation of man's ability to realize his individuality and experience authenticity even in the face of deprivation and disaster. Conscious of art as a mode of celebrating life, he finds it a source of affirmation. This sense of affirmation, in its turn, is the informing spirit of all his writing. Thus his fiction is pervaded by the positive, making his novels imaginative creations of man as acquiring authenticity and acceptance, in a world characterized by spiritual sterility, alienation and absurdity. Denying the general emphasis on the negative, Malamud demonstrates a faith that Max Schulz describes as "Radical Sophistication." This, Schulz asserts, is the peculiar characteristic of the Jew, for, "this willingness to accept the world on its own terms—disorderly, incoherent, absurd . . . and yet without losing faith in the moral significance of human action, underlies the confrontation of experience in the best of contemporary Jewish American novels."[26] Thus Malamud demonstrates the possibilities of bringing order and peace into a world riddled with chaos and strife.

Malamud's method of presenting this message follows an interesting line of development. *The Fixer*, his fourth novel, occupies a central position, for it divides the novels into two sections—those that precede it and those that succeed it. Beginning with *The Natural*, each novel presents the protagonist as developing and entering into more meaningful experience, until it reaches *The Fixer*. In the first four novels, the protagonist begins at the negative end, as a victim of external forces distraught with feeling of despair and loneliness. But Malamud does not leave him there, for ultimately he follows a pattern of recovery. Thus from the negative sense of being a mere puppet of forces unknown to him, having little if any power of choice and self-direction, Malamud's protagonist, Roy Hobbs, Frank Alpine, S. Levin and Yakov Bok, develops into a unique, complete man, bearing the dignity and responsibility of an individual.

Malamud fixes on the actuality of the person as an individual, making him conscious of his existence as unique. It is then, and only then, implies Malamud, that man can relate to himself and others. Thus, the moment of experience that begins the journey of the Malamudian hero toward meaning and affirmation is a crucial moment, he must experience. In *The Assistant*, the moment when Frank Alpine discovers the meaninglessness and emptiness of his actions performed automatically, is a moment of dramatic revelation: "One day while he [Alpine] lay in some hole he had crawled into . . . a whole lot different . . . different."[27] This was the moment when Alpine confronted reality and took the initial step in his journey towards commitment and responsibility. A more brilliant presentation of similar experience is found in *A New Life* when S. Levin confronted reality: "One morning in somebody's filthy cellar—I then became a man of principle."[28] This disclosure or absurdity of existence is a crucial moment in the life of Malamud's protagonist, for it opens him to his being. This consciousness is the source of his freedom, impressing on him that he is responsible for his existence. Consequently, Levin is conscious of a new identity for, "what was new were my plans for myself,"[29] he tells Pauline. Existence is perceived as having a value of its own, making the protagonist exercise a choice, irrevocable and self-respecting. This moment, crucial to his existence, places him on the road to meaning and significance. The theme of love begins at this point, the development of the protagonist from self-regard towards a life of commitment. In realizing his uniqueness and responsibility as an individual, the protagonist moves towards affirmation. Thereafter, following a pattern of recovery, Malamud's protagonist infuses his life with significance.

The moral development of the protagonist that we witness in the earlier novels gains maturity in Malamud's fourth novel *The Fixer*. Malamud asserts that this novel is not a case study when he says: "A case study couldn't be art. . . . I'll tell you this: if the book isn't about freedom, I don't know what it is about."[30] Like all Malamud's former protagonists we meet Yakov Bok when he is about to leave the *Shtetl* in quest of better possibilities abroad.

He begins his journey with arrogance and self-centredness when he says: "It's time to get out and take a chance. Change your place your luck, people say."[31] While in Malamud's earlier novels, the theme of responsibility and acceptance was restricted to the protagonist's own personal circle, with *A New Life*, we see the sphere widening. S. Levin takes upon himself the responsibility of creating a liberal atmosphere in college. Yakov, though initially self-centred, grows to bear the burden of responsibility for the whole race, in fact, of all the suppressed and suffering masses of Russia. In the end we see Yakov on the way to the court for trial. Whether Yakov is acquitted or sentenced is of little importance, for what Malamud was interested in was to trace the growth of man in adverse conditions. Yakov grows morally strong in his struggle to establish the innocence of his persecuted race.

In *The Tenants*, Malamud portrays the cultural nihilism and despair of our dehumanized age in all its stark nakedness. Here, we can discern that the sense of optimism and staunch faith in the possibilities of man that Malamud had demonstrated from *The Natural* to *The Fixer* seems to have been displaced by an enervating pessimism and some loss of faith, as Malamud has confessed, "Yes, My faith in humanity has bruised to some degree."[32] In *The Tenants*, Malamud does not evade the nightmarish reality of modern experience, but by confronting its irrationality, he hopes to use that experience for the purpose of emphasizing the need to overcome the despairing reality and to establish brotherhood. *The Tenants*, true to form, emphasizes the value of brotherhood and community despite the denigration of human life in modern society. "If life, as it is, offers cause for despair and if the individual is both product and producer of this life, then the individual must be redeemed. Through his redemption society will be redeemed."[33] And the stress is on the need for redemption as achieved through love for others. To selflessly love another is to achieve great heights in Malamud's fiction. But as Malamud has said, "Every one can't give love, one the mature man or woman can do it. . . . Love in essence enlarges the self. Find and give what you can in love."[34] Malamud's characters live in a world of interpersonal relationships and as per Malamud's norms the protagonist needs to realize and fulfil obligations to others in order to achieve authenticity and acceptance.

The protagonist of *The Tenants*, Lesser is an isolated individual living in a prison of his own making. Like Morris Bober of *The Assistant* was in the grocery store, Lesser lives entombed in the tenement. He does not feel the need to communicate or give or talk with the world around him. He tries to convince the landlord, Levenspiel, that his novel, if he can bring it to a conclusion of ideal love, will help Levenspiel to "understand and endure"[35] his own life. Lesser's insulated life style gets shattered by Willie Spearmint, a writer aspirant who comes to share Lesser's empty tenement. From a position of detachment and mutual fear, they move towards undefined feelings resembling brotherhood. Their common passion of writing brings them together. *The Tenants* is most representative of Malamud's creative and technical originality. The hatred and violence which form the reality of the novel only heightens the readers' consciousness of the postulate of love. Thus, what seems to be Malamud's loss of faith in humanity, is, in fact, a new fictional method for propagating the struggle for recognition.

*Dubin's Lives* has been considered as "Malamud's simplest novel since *A New Life* and may be his most affecting."[36] All of Malamud's earlier novels spoke of moral possibilities of man through purgative suffering and selfless love. His latter novels, however, seem to fall outside the sphere of suffering and moral accountability. The real subject of *Dubin's Lives* is a "life battling with itself and effects of time . . . the affecting of aging, the loneliness and paralysis of a long marriage, the desire for a new life."[37] The undercurrents of pessimism that ran throughout *The Tenants* is there also in *Dubin's Lives*. Thus, once again we deal with Malamud's basic premises, that is to say, the protagonist's struggle for self-assertion and search for a new life and the way to it—by striking a balance between the opposing of private desires and selfless commitment towards others. Dubin, the protagonist of *Dubin's Lives*, is the new activist hero. He is "an intrepid opportunist of the self. He is eager, insatiable explorer of his own private experience, always on the alert, in Augie March's phrase for 'a fate good enough.'"[38] Dubin seeks escape from the stagnation of his everyday existence and for a personally meaningful identity. When we first meet him his real concern is for his life in totality. The problem he creates for himself make him despair: "what a mad thing to happen. What a fool I am. . . . I'm like a broken clock—works, time, mingled. What is life trying to teach me?"[39] Dubin has to learn to accept the dilapidation that time has wrought and in late middle age he should not hope to recover his youth. He suffers, as do all Malamud's heroes. His suffering is the outcome of his own blundering desires. Dubin suffers because he is not a mench but a man with many weaknesses and failings. In Dubin, we see an individual's existential situation as an isolated being seeking meaning in life. The only way he can transcend the universal chaos that surround him and forge a private identity is by way of love, compassion and moral commitment towards others.

From the realistic setting of *Dubin's Lives*, Malamud moves to fantasy in *God's Grace*. It is a prophetic allegory, predicting apocalypse as a dread possibility of the near future. Calvin Cohn broods over his fate as lone survivor of all humanity after the Devastation. Encouraged by his discovery of another living being, Malamud's protagonist sets out to create a new life for himself as the past has come to nothing. "Survive is what we have to do. Thus we protest our fate to God and at the same time imitate Him,"[40] Cohn thinks. He tells Buz, "My father said survival was one way we shared God's purpose."[41] He reconciles to God's will, and is indeed grateful for small mercies. In *God's Grace*, the primates not only talk; each has a telling name and distinctive traits. Malamud gives them an individuality which does credit to the author's creative ability.

Therefore, contrary to the modern trend in fiction of regression and devaluation of man, Bernard Malamud writes parables of man's capabilities to redeem himself. Well aware of the dubious lot of man in the present-day impersonal world, Malamud still declines to accept the defeat of the human spirit in an individual. Man suffers no doubt, but by making a few adjustments to the world he can still find modes of recognition, moments of acceptance and authenticity.

## NOTES

1. Qtd. Ben Siegel, "Through a Glass Darkly: Bernard Malamud's Painful Views of the Self," Richard Astro and Jackson J. Benson, ed., *The Fiction of Bernard Malamud* (Cornvallis: Oregon State Univ. Press, 1977) 122.
2. Haskel Frankel, "Interview with Bernard Malamud," *Saturday Review*, 49 (September 10, 1966) 40.
3. Joseph Wershba, "Not Horror but Sadness," *The New York Post* (September 14, 1958) 3.
4. Marjorie Dent Candes, ed., *Current Biography Year Book* (New York: Routledge, 1958) 272.
5. Daniel Stern, "The Art of Fiction: Bernard Malamud," *Paris Review*, 61 (Spring 1975) 62.
6. Ruth R. Wisse, *The Schlemiel as Modern Hero* (Chicago: Univ. of Chicago Press, 1971) 93.
7. Qtd. W.J. Handy, "The Malamud Hero: A Quest for Existence," Astro and Benson, ed., *The Fiction of Bernard Malamud*, 65.
8. Rep. Granville Hicks, "Literary Horizons," *Saturday Review*, 47 (October 12, 1963) 32.
9. David Boroff, "Lossers, But Not Lost," *Saturday Review*, 47 (October 12, 1963) 33.
10. Irving and Harriet Deer, "Philip Roth and the Crisis in American Fiction," *Minnesota Review*, 6 (1966) 353.
11. Katha Pollit, "Creators on Creating: Bernard Malamud," *Saturday Review* (February 24, 1981) 39.
12. Daniel Stern, 61.
13. Marcus Klein, *After Alienation: American Novel in Mid-Century* (New York: World Book Publishing, 1965) 252.
14. Ruth B. Mandel, "Bernard Malamud's *The Assistant* and *A New Life*: Ironic Affirmation," *Critique*, 7 (1964-65) 11.
15. Irving Howe, "Mass Society and Post-Modern Fiction," Joseph J. Waldmeir, ed., *Recent American Fiction: Some Critical Views* (Boston: Bacon Press, 1963) 13.
16. Mark Goldman, "Bernard Malamud's Comic Vision and the Theme of Identity," *Critique*, 7: 2 (Winter 1964-65) 93.
17. Ihab Hassan, *Radical Innocence: Studies in the Contemporary American Novel* (New Jersey: Princeton Univ. Press, 1961) 161.

18. Robert Alter, "Sentimentalizing the Jew," *Commentary*, 40: 3 (1965) 74.
19. Ruth B. Mandel, 111.
20. Robert Alter, 35.
21. Ralph Tyler, "A Talk with the Novelist," *New York Times Book Review*, 84 (February 18, 1979) 34.
22. E.H. Leelavathi Masilamoni, "Bernard Malamud—An Interview," *Indian Journal of American Studies*, 9 (1979) 33.
23. Philip Roth, "Writing American Fiction," *Reading Myself and B thers* (New York: Straus, Farrar and Giroux, 1975) 127.
24. Ruth R. Wisse, 10.
25. Daniel L. Stevenson, "The Activists," *Daedalus*, 92 (1963) 238.
26. Max F. Schulz, *Radical Sophistication: Studies in Contemporary Oewish-American Fiction* (Athens: Ohio Univ. Press, 1969) 22.
27. Bernard Malamud, *The Assistant* (Harmondsworth: Penguin, 1967) 84.
28. Bernard Malamud, *A New Life* (New York: Avon, 1980) 175.
29. *Ibid*., 177.
30. Haskel Frankel, 39.
31. Bernard Malamud, *The Fixer* (Harmondsworth: Penguin, 1968) 15.
32. E.H. Leelavathi Masilamoni, 36.
33. John Jacob Clayton, *Saul Bellow: In Defence of Man* (Bloomington: Indiana Univ. Press, 1968) 5.
34. E.H. Leelavathi Masilamoni, 35.
35. Bernard Malamud, *The Tenants* (Harmondsworth: Penguin, 1971) 22.
36. G.W. Hunt, "Bernard Malamud," *Atlantic*, 243 (1979) 132.
37. Pearl K. Bell, "Heller and Malamud: Time and Now," *Commentary*, 67 (1979) 73.
38. David L. Stevenson, 238.
39. Bernard Malamud, *Dubin's Lives* (Harmondsworth: Penguin, 1979) 162.
40. Bernard Malamud, *God's Grace* (Harmondsworth: Penguin, 1982) 82.
41. *Ibid.*

## Jewish Dilemma

Although there were Jewish-American novelists of great distinction in the first two decades of the twentieth century, they did not gain as much prominence as the novelists of the nineteen thirties. But even these novelists could never have imagined the success and immense popularity enjoyed by the novelists of the nineteen sixties. Even in the mid-seventies the Jewish-American novelists continued to flourish with the major ones being Saul Bellow, Bernard Malamud, Philip Roth, Norman Mailer and J.D. Salinger. Besides these, other important American novelists among the Jews are Herbert Gold, Bruce Freedman, Leslie Fiedler, Herman Wuork, Leon Uris and Jerome Weidman.

All these Jewish-American writers together have created "an important body of work, a good deal of high critical as well as of popular acclaim."[1] However, it is debatable whether this "important body of work" could be described as a movement in contemporary American fiction. Conflicting views have been expressed by the critics on this matter. While one critic supporting the idea of the movement says, "only those too perverse or fuzzy-headed to recognize cultural facts now refuse to acknowledge the existence of a Jewish movement in contemporary American writing and especially the writing of fiction,"[2] the other refuting the idea observes that just as "there was no lake school of English poets in 1810 . . . there is no Jewish school of novelists now. There are only Jewish-American writers practicing their craft."[3]

Whether these writers are linked together in a movement or not, they undoubtedly enjoy unprecedented popularity today. How does one explain this mass appeal of Jewish-American writers? It is difficult to adduce the actual grounds of their appeal since several reasons have been advanced in this respect.

More often than not, it is the Jewishness of these writers that has been considered to be the major factor of their appeal. Leslie Fiedler has very aptly put forward this idea:

> We live at a moment when everywhere in the realm of prose Jewish writers have discovered their Jewishness to be an eminently marketable commodity, their much-vaunted alienation to be their passport into the heart of Gentile American culture.[4]

This observation of Fiedler seems to be close to truth since the Jewish-American writers willingly or otherwise exploit their Jewishness for their creative efforts. Even the most assimilated of these writers cannot escape making use of his Jewishness in his writings. In this context, it is significant to note Robert Alter's remarks:

> It is by no means clear what sense is to be made of the Jewishness of a writer who neither uses a unique Jewish language, nor describes literary traditions that are recognizably Jewish . . . one can't however simply discount the possibility that some essentially Jewish quality may adhere to the writing of the most thoroughly accultured Jews.[5]

It is this "essentially Jewish quality" which has become a distinct commercial success. However, this quality alone does not lead these writers to the prestigious position they occupy today. As Malin has observed, these writers tend to produce 'powerful' and 'sincere' literature only when they "are directly concerned with their Jewishness, otherwise they offer less intense, phony, or imperfect work."[6] Malin supports this argument by citing example from the works of Bellow, Malamud and Roth: "Roth is weaker in *Letting Go* than in 'Eli, the Fanatic'; Bellow is weaker in *Augie March* than in *Seize the Day* or *The Victim*; Malamud is weaker in *The Natural* than in *The Assistant*."[7]

Any attempt at defining the term 'Jewishness' leads to the baffling question: what is a Jew? This question has perplexed not only non-Jews but the Jews themselves. A great deal of writing has been done to answer it but no standard or clear-cut definition has been arrived at so far.

The early Jews defined themselves as an ethnic group, the seed of Abraham. Therefore, anyone born of Jewish parents was considered to be a Jew. But as things stand today, not all the Jews of the world are the lineal descendants of Abraham. This naturally precludes any definition of Jews as a race. Similarly not all the Jews of the world profess a common religion. While it is true that the majority of Jews believe in Judaism as their religion, there are many converts from Judaism to other faiths who consider themselves Jews in spite of their conversion. This falsifies any definition of Jewishness as religion. In the Diaspora, the Jews have acquired different cultural traits in different parts of the world and taken up different nationalities. Hence, a cultural and national definition of Jewishness is also not correct. Thus, the Jews cannot define themselves exclusively in terms of race, religion, nation or even a culture. This then raises a very pertinent question: If Jewishness is not a matter of faith, race, nation or culture, what, then, is it? Jean-Paul Sartre thinks that Jews do not exist. They are simply the creation of anti-Semites:

> What is it, then, that serves to keep a semblance of unity in the Jewish community? To reply to this question, we must come back to the idea of situation. It is neither their past, their religion, nor their soul that unites the sons of Israel. If they have a common bond, if all of them deserve the name of Jew, it is because they have in common the situation of a Jew, that is, they live in a community which takes them for Jews.[8]

This is known as the politics of position and is relevant to the Diasporic writings. Just as a Jew for Sartre is a 'reflection of non-Jewish attitudes,' so also for Shapiro, Jewishness is defined only in relation to its environment. Paul Luther has explained Shapiro's belief: "in a non-Jewish world the Jew is looked upon, whatever he may choose to become, as a Jew—an atheist Jew, a Catholic Jew but always a Jew."[9] The validity of this observation is seen by the fact that Karl Marx is considered by everyone to have been a Jew in spite of the fact that he was born in a family that had embraced Christianity. Similarly the Nazis picked up for genocide even those highly assimilated nominal German Jews who were ignorant of the fundamentals of Judaism and Jewish history.

Ernest Van den Haag seems to have taken into consideration all those aspects of the problem before arriving at his own definition of Jewishness: "a man's feeling that he is, like it or not, Jewish makes him a Jew. This feeling even when ambiguous, even when unconscious, often makes others feel so, too regardless of denial, conversion, or apostasy. . . . This feeling can't be willed."[10] Mordecai M. Kaplan also defines Jewishness as a feeling:

> A people is a group of human beings whose ancestors once lived together, and who have developed a we-feeling which is transmitted from one generation to the next. We-feeling results from living together and acting in common in the furtherance of shared interest . . . it is the 'we-feeling' the sense which Jews have of mutual belongingness.[11]

After having surveyed these attempts at defining of Jew one cannot but agree with sociologist Louis Wirth who thinks: "We cannot really define a Jew except to say that a Jew is a person who thinks of himself as a Jew and who is treated by others as if he were a Jew."[12] This is a definition which embraces all the other definitions of a Jew. Any one who considers himself a Jew either on account of his prominent Jewish descent or because of his belief in Judaism is a Jew. Similarly, any one who carries in him the cultural traits of the European *Shtetl* or who feels a sense of oneness with all the other Jews of the world, is a Jew.

Just as it is difficult to define a Jew in precise terms, so it is difficult to list Jewish characteristics. However, it is possible to sort out certain traits which are common among Jews despite the fact that they have been scattered among alien cultures for hundreds of years. Religion occupies a prominent place in the lives of most of the Jews. For Judaism is an all-pervasive norm of conduct and regulation of daily activity. Secondly, there is a sense of peoplehood among all the Jews of the world which transcends the social, cultural, economic and national boundaries. Thirdly, to be a Jew means following numerous traditional "rules of conduct about eating, marrying, intercourse, children, education about almost every detail of life."[13] The Jewish traits can thus be summed up in the words of Ernest Van den Haag: "To be a Jewish is to cling to a set of practices and rituals, sacred and profane, to a set of activities and institutions, religious and secular, to a set of attitudes more than to any elaborate beliefs."[14]

It is precisely these sets of 'practices' and 'attitudes' and 'rules of conduct' which bring the Jews into conflict with the Americans. The American Jew is thus torn between two sets of values—the American and the Jewish. These two sets of values also represent forces of groups' survival and those of integration and acceptance into American society. This phenomenon is neither new nor unique to the Jews. In the past, even outside America, wherever the Jews lived, they suffered from this dilemma. If, on the one hand, they were attracted by non-Jewish values and desired acceptance by the Gentile society, on the other, they wanted group identity and survival as a distinct community.

One of the early demands on the Jewish settlers in America was made by the 'melting pot' theory. This concept of America as a melting pot came from Zangwill's popular play by the same name. According to this theory America was a cauldron into which all racial and cultural strains of immigrants were to be poured and blended to form a new nation. In order to Americanize in this manner, the immigrants were encouraged to discard their traditional customs and rituals and prompted to take on the external forms of American life, ignoring the deep moral and spiritual differences between the American and the minority group. The supporters of this theory believed it that once the immigrants jumped into the pot and went through the cooking process, they would come out as thoroughly assimilated Americans.

The 'melting pot' theory has come in for attack recently from all quarters. It is now realized that America does not demand uniformity. One of the serious flaws of the 'melting pot' theory was the idea that all groups who come to America must divest themselves of former traditions and cultural heritage in order not to be distinguished from the mainstream. Many noted

American social thinkers have questioned the validity of this idea and pointed out that the American culture and society can be better served if the minorities are allowed to retain their identity and distinct culture. Americanization, according to Bogords, "means giving the immigrant the best America has to offer and retaining for America the best in the immigrant."[15]

The survivalists among the Jews vehemently repudiated the idea of abandoning one's group identity and cultural heritage. They assert that following one's own religion or even fostering it is not against the spirit of American democracy. Morris Raphael Cohen states:

> The idea that all immigrants should wipe out their past and become simple imitations of the existing types is neither possible nor desirable. The past cannot be wiped out. And we make ourselves ridiculous in an effort to do so. . . . All great civilizations, have been the results of the contribution of many people and a richer American culture can come only if the Jews like other elements are given a chance to develop under favourable conditions their peculiar genius.[16]

Mordecai M. Kaplan has pointed out that the American democracy today provides the opportunity for Jews to retain their group life within the general American society. They are no longer forced to become one with the rest. Yet, the American Jew is torn between the forces of integration and group survival. If he faces this dilemma it is not because of any external pressures on him but his own inherent ambivalence. The representative Jew, whatever position he takes on the integration-survival scale, is pulled in both directions. He desires that he must be treated as an equal and that his Jewishness should not be taken into account in any judgement the society passes over him. But at the same time he wants full acceptance as an American but in certain matters like inter-marriage he takes a very rigid and communal stand. No position at either end of the integration-survival scale is acceptable to him. In fact, the majority of the Jews are not interested in either of these positions. A typical Jew is more anxious to find an ideological position which denies the existence of any tension between survival and integration. Trying to reconcile these two incompatible positions, he remains a problem to himself. As for the Jew who has made his choice as an assimilationist or survivalist, there appears to be no problem.

A significant aspect of the Jewish-American life is that even the most thoroughly acculturated of Jews in America suffers from the same dilemma of being a Jew on the one hand and an American on the other. The reason is quite simple: the Jewish and American values clash with each other in the same person as Malin states, "the Jew and the American confront each other often in the same person."[17]

The resultant strained condition in which the American Jew finds himself is very correctly described by Emmanuel Feldman:

> One of the paradoxes of the American Jew is the fact that despite his freedom and his ever widening vistas of opportunity, he lives under a nameless tension. In a country which offers him freedom to live as he desires he is basically ill at ease. In an environment which permits him to live, act and think as his non-Jewish neighbour does, the Jew beneath the facade of apparent conformity, is not completely comfortable. Even as he conforms to the patterns of American life he feels himself the perpetual outsider.[18]

The fundamental reason for this paradoxical position of the American Jew, according to Feldman, "is the divergence between what is characteristically Jewish and that which is characteristically American, a polarity of views which cannot quite be reconciled."[19] He has very convincingly pointed out some of the key differences between the Jewish and the American, the most obvious being between the two traditions of 'national origins.' Whereas the American tradition dates back to a mere two hundred years, the Jewish tradition is as old as history itself. Hence, the archetypal American has "no deep sense of history, going back when the patriotic occasion demands only to founding fathers and the constitution."[20] On the other hand, for the archetypal Jew a deep sense of history is imbibed in his consciousness. His religion, Judaism, is a "religion of history, a religion of time. The God of Israel was not found primarily in the facts of nature. He spoke through events in history."[21]

This obvious difference between the time span of the two histories has led to 'disparate time-view' and 'dissimilar world-view' held both by the Jews and the Americans. Unlike the American, the Jew is more patient since he has time. The notion of achieving anything through short cuts is totally alien to him. Since the Americans are comparatively rootless they have lesser respect for tradition than the Jews. Harold Laski says, "The characteristic American is always on the move. He is always willing to try something new. He is skeptical of anything that expresses itself as permanent and absolute."[22] The Americans are obsessed with newness and experiment. Here, Malin strikes a note of warning when he says that "the American has become so obsessed with newness that he forgets the power of the past, and the Jewish concern only for the past can lead to present maladjustment."[23]

Another notable difference between the American and the Jew is of the differing sets of values and contrary approaches to the realm of thought. There is little of mystery or symbolism in American life as a result of its clear, factual and documented history. "The American spirit is the song of the open road: the past is known, the future charted."[24] This cannot be said of the Jew for he is "rooted in something less open and tangible. His beginning and his destiny are shrouded in the unknown and Jewish life is replete with symbol, with ritual, and with mystery."[25] Because of the unambiguous nature of its tradition and history, feels Feldman, American thought is 'concrete and pragmatic.' A typical American, therefore, is a doer rather than a thinker. Conversely, Jewish thought is abstract and unutilitarian.

Closely linked with the concept of time are the concepts of Exile and family life for Jews. The past reminds the Jew of the Holy Land which traditionally is the Promised Land for them. Since the majority of the Jews believe in the promise given to them by God, they consider themselves aliens in America, even if they have been born and brought up here. Thus they are faced with the baffling question whether they should consider America as their home or Diaspora. The more they think in terms of Israel, the more they suffer from the tension between homeland and Exile.

Not only are the American Jews troubled by the conflict of the American and the Jew within themselves, their beliefs, customs and rituals are threatened by the overriding influence of Americanism. The American society as a whole possesses a danger to their values and systems. It is natural for the Jewish writer in America to reflect the tensions, dilemmas and problems of his people in his writings. Writing about the Jewish-American novelists, Ihab Hassan observes:

> Anxious and ambivalent, he often expresses tensions of skepticism and belief, assimilation and identity, new mixed marriage and old family manners, in complex forms. An ancient equilibrist of pain and humour, scapegoat and pariah, he sees in his condition a symbol not retrograde, but prophetic of the human condition.[26]

The Jewish-American novelists, consciously or unconsciously, deal with the Jewish experience in America. However, it is true that they are not always exclusively concerned with the Jewish experience. America gives freedom to these writers to deal with any subject they like. The Jewish-American writers are drawn in two opposite directions. On the one hand, they desire to describe their experiences as Jews, on the other, they wish to be regarded as American writers, writing for the Americans. While some writers resolve this dilemma by concentrating on Jewish themes, others voice their Jewishness in different ways through non-Jewish themes. Some like Mailer, Bellow or Salinger accept no restriction on their material, and a few like Malamud write mainly about Jewishness, yet manage to transcend the narrow limits of their subject.

The Jewish-American writer, like the typical American Jew, experiences the tension between the old and new generation, between ghetto and suburb, bar mitzval and little league baseball, synagogue and college, gabardine and ivy-league suits. This tension spurs "the Jewish writer to an evaluation of his heritage as a Jew, American and modern man."[27] That is to say, he creates out of the experience of modern American Jew not only a portrait of the American but also a picture of universal human condition. Out of the tension resulting from "the conflict of contrary loyalties and the desire to resolve it into meaningful order, he produces, occasionally great art."[28]

Malamud's protagonists are avowedly Jews but they live detached from the social and religious experience of Jewish communal life. Robert Alter is quick to point out the absence of a Jewish milieu in Malamud's novels when he says: "that a Jewish community never enters into his books except as a shadow of a vestige of a spectre."[29] Philip Roth points out that Malamud has not made the contemporary scene a backdrop for his writing:

> The Jews of *The Magic Barrel* and the Jews of *The Assistant*, I have reason to suspect, are not the Jews of New York City or Chicago. . . . Malamud, as a writer of fiction, has not shown specific interest in the anxieties and dilemmas and corruptions of modern American Jew, the Jew we think of as characteristic of our time; rather. his people live in a timeless depression and a placeless Lower East Side.[30]

In some way Malamud's Jews seem to belong to the East European *Shtetl*. And yet Malamud's protagonists differ from their East European forbears in that they do not have a cultural and communal tradition based upon the adherence to Talmudic principles as did the old world Jews. Comparing them with Sholom Aleichem's characters, Sam Bluefarb points out that though Malamud's characters are still, to some extent, composed of the Old World content, yet they have also taken on the New World form and "have become, if not completely assimilated, then—after a fashion, 'naturalized.'"[31] At any rate, the Jewish identity of the Malamudian hero has lost its religious and ethnic content. In fact, his Jewishness is largely symbolic.

In Malamud's first novel *The Natural*, its protagonist and milieu are not Jewish. This has led to some critics to feel that this novel is "uncharacteristic of Malamud,"[32] but its obvious concern with the theme of man's quest for identity, self-assertion, acceptance and the efficiency of suffering as the means of realizing it, makes it amply clear that the novel "belongs to a pattern of development which has been consistent from first to last."[33]

The apparent peculiarity of *The Natural* when considered as a part of Malamud's works, is an indication of his refusal to play safe by choosing only Jewish themes. He makes baseball, the popular American sport, his vehicle for the exploration of contemporary man's quest for identity.

*The Natural* is much more than a baseball story. It delineates Roy's quest for recognition in organized baseball which is the external projection of his inner urge for acceptance and identity. There is a gap between Roy's inner urges and his conscious goals, which he fails to perceive and, Malamud succeeds in dramatizing the struggle of his protagonist to overcome his limitations and achieve identity as an individual.

In an impromptu contest besides the railway tracks on the outskirts of a city, the rising young god strikes out 'Whammer' the best batter of the day. Harriet Bird, "a snoppy goddess,"[34] in black, hails his victory. For his narcissistic longings and overwhelming pride, Roy is struck down by Harriet in a "mythic enactment of the psychic wound,"[35] with a silver bullet in his guts. Roy, as are all Malamud's heroes, is caught in "an ethical dilemma of American life."[36] One aspect of the dilemma is obvious in Roy's ambition to be the greatest—the natural outcome of the prevalent American values though undoubtedly selfish and narrow. Harriet projects the other aspect of the dilemma—the need to transcend the earthly desires and aspire for more glorious ends. These distinctively divergent attitudes, the selfish and benign are explicit in Roy's own self and as he makes his choice between these two attitudes, he experiences a moral struggle. The conflict, within one self, which the protagonist undergoes as he learns to distinguish between the right and wrong is basic to *The Natural* as well as to the rest of Malamud's fiction. Roy's fate is so much like that of Malamud's Jews—his suffering and his possible redemption through selfless involvement with others that one realizes what Malamud means when he says, "All men are Jews . . . although few men know it."[37] Roy, though not a Jew, is not unlike Malamud's latter heroes who are Jews mostly in name and by birth. Roy shares with the other protagonists their fate of misfortune and ill-luck. However, Malamud's constant attempt is to project both the necessity and the possibility of growth in man. His journey begun with blind egoism ends in mature self-understanding.

*The Assistant* is different from *The Natural* in tone and milieu, but demonstrates Malamud's continuing interest in man's struggle for acceptance and authenticity. In *The Natural*, Malamud had projected the dualities which operate within man and how awareness of one's weakness leads to the possibility of overcoming them, thus, promising a less painful future. Malamud personally feels:

> After completing my first novel, *The Natural*, in essence mythic, I wanted to do a more serious, deeper, perhaps, realistic piece of work. The apprentice character interested me, as he has in much of my fiction, the man who, as much he can in the modern world, is in the process of changing his fate his life. This sort of person, not at all complicated, appears for the first time in my writing in the short story 'The First Seven Years' . . . and I thought, I would like to develop the possibilities of his type.[38]

Likewise, "in his guilt-wracked efforts to escape the determinism of his own past and the countering claims of the will, the assistant confronts on almost every level, but in a new dimension, the same cycle of experience that shapes the morality of *The Natural*."[39] The protagonist of *The Assistant* Frank Alpine is aware of the conflicting impulses from the very beginning. The novel is a probing study of a weak man's painful endeavour to become a strong, principled man. Though the story is of a Gentile's conversion into a Jew, it is not about Judaism. It is simply a story of one man's efforts to change himself into a better person. From a petty thief and an undisciplined person he struggles to be honest and responsible one. The novel is "an affirmation of man's ability to realize himself even in the face of deprivation and disaster."[40]

Just as Roy travels east with the high hope that he is due for something big, Frank Alpine is a drifter without a home and values, and "his life was mostly made up of lost chances."[41] His old life having come to nothing, Frank seeks to start afresh with a new self and a new moral consciousness. He must acknowledge his past mistakes and atone for them. He must discipline himself.

Frank Alpine desires a 'new life' yet, being still an undisciplined person, looks for it by becoming a criminal. He feels, "he would change his luck, make adventure, live like a prince. He shivered with pleasure as he conceived robberies, assaults . . . each violent act helping to satisfy a craving that somebody suffer as his own fortune improved" (84). This is how he comes to gang up with Ward Minogue, who own a flourishing liquor store in the neighbourhood, to rob the Jew's grocery store. During the hold up when Ward hits the hapless Jew, Frank realizes that he has "made the worst mistake yet, the hardest to wipe out," and "his plans of crime lay down and died" (85). He suffers pangs of guilt and to quiet his conscience he goes back to the grocery to work for its Jewish owner, Morris Bober. For penitence he becomes Morris's 'assistant' without pay. He won't stay there long, he promises himself, "I'm only staying there till I figure out what's my next move" (88). While Morris lies in bed, recuperating from the injury, Frank makes sincere efforts to increase the income of the grocery. The grocery becomes the avenue of his slow and painful change for the better. The two factors which get Frank going on the right path are his own guilty conscience at having robbed Morris, and the grocers's kindness towards him when he lay starving and frozen in the cellar.

On the symbolic level, the characters in the novel are the archetypes of the good and evil aspects of Frank's personality. It is through his relationship with the other characters that Frank learns to overcome his weak self and assert his moral self. His association with Ward Minogue, Morris Bober and Helen help him achieve self-perception and thus develop from egoistic preoccupations to commitment towards others. Ward is the archetypal symbol of his evil self. The only good outcome of Frank's interaction with ward is that he begins to recognize the evil aspect of his psyche and in a bid to reject the evil in his nature Frank breaks off from Ward and turns towards Morris and Helen. Both father and daughter will be instrumental in altering his attitude towards others and in becoming a better person himself.

In Morris Bober, Frank finds such goodness and poverty as he had admired in St. Francis. Frank is attracted by Morris's endurance of all hardships that befall him, his acceptance of his fate and above all his kind compassion for others—all the legendary virtues associated with the Jew. Morris in the role of guide to 'apprentice' hero demonstrates such qualities which Frank will adopt once he begins to reform.

Morris Bober is the *schlemiel* figure of the Jewish folk tradition. He has a talent for attracting bad luck. Morris is inept and unfortunate and, therefore, "his troubles grew like bananas in bunches" (134). He suffers many indignities but he accepts everything with resignation. Morris's wholehearted charity is obvious in the way he extends credit to his customers even when he can ill-afford to do so. As always, his goodness of heart overpowers his practical resolve to be tougher in demanding repayment. "Obviously, kindness or generosity makes man vulnerable and ashamed."[42] Amidst surrounding degradation and dishonesty, Morris stands out for his humanity.

Frank genuinely admires such goodness in Morris but continues to be bad himself. "He is like a man with two minds" (110)—an unintegrated man. His good impulses clash constantly with his bad ones. "He is not bad; it is only that he finds it prohibitively difficult to be as good as he would wish—a saint's good. This is the essential paradox of his existence: he meant to do good yet compulsively continues to do harm."[43] Frank has become the grocer's assistant out of guilt for his part in robbing and assaulting Morris. He continues to be an assistant because he goes on to add to the burden of his guilt by his misdoing. "Guilt of imperfection (the presumption of the romantic hero), he debases himself as penance. . . . Since he wants more than anything else to be a good man, his crimes are a means of self-punishment. Each time he pockets money from Morris's register, he torments himself with guilt."[44] Thus, we see that he indulges his weak self and torments himself. He lives in "a climate of regret" (17), and yet cannot restrict his evil and good actions, and is willing to improve himself; these, in itself, make his redemption possible.

Besides all this, Frank stays on because under the good influence of Morris, he begins to change. At first, Frank is repelled by the Jewish way of life. His prejudice against the Jews surfaces now and then, "That's what they live for, Frank thought, to suffer" (81). His unfavourable attitude towards the suffering grocer is emphasized, when he says, "They were born prisoners. That was what Morris was, with his deadly patience, or endurance, or whatever the hell it was" (79). Though unhappy at Morris's condition, Frank is attracted by Morris's attitude towards his life. Before long, Frank graduates from disgust to curiosity about the Jews. He questions Morris closely about the Jewish religion for he feels that it was Morris's Jewishness which teaches him to accept suffering like a martyr. Frank's sensibility has always been drawn towards Jewish idealism, though it takes time for him to realize that. In fact, as Marcus Klein says, "Malamud has himself spoken of the similarity of sensibilities he finds existing between Italians and Jews."[45]

To Frank's insistent queries about Jews, Morris explains: "to be a Jew all you need is a good heart" (112). Morris is not a Jew in the traditional sense for he does not follow any of the Jewish rituals and customs. The rabbi in *The Assistant* declares that there are many ways to be a Jew, and he considers Morris Bober to be true Jew, notwithstanding his neglect of formal traditions, "because he lived in the Jewish heart" (203). For such reasons, he tells us, Bober is a Jew even though he disregarded the Law and failed to attend the Synagogue. Morris followed the spirit of Judaism, not all its rules. Even then, it is not his religion, but suffering and endurance, that defines Morris as a Jew. Anybody who suffers and endures all willingly and with hope in the future, is a Jew and this brings us to Malamud's statement that 'all men are Jews.'

It is only after Morris's death that Frank experiences resurrection and his life passes from a spiritual fulfilment. Frank starts as the Jewish grocer's apprentice; he ends as the Jewish grocer himself. His identification with Morris is complete; he takes over the responsibility of his store and along with it Morris's fate of suffering.

In *A New Life*, Malamud shows his continuing concern with modern man's search for authenticity and acceptance on the social and emotional levels. An interesting fact that relates this novel to the American culture is that its protagonist retraces in his Westward journey the frontier myth within the Jewish-American pattern. Despite the fact that the world of this novel is close to contemporary America, it explores, like the earlier novels, man's quest for his selfhood and acceptance in a world that denies him these.

Like Roy and Frank, S. Levin is in quest of integration, but is more articulate and aware of his intellectual training. His disaffection from his past and alienation from society are prominent features of Levin's personality at the beginning. There is nothing overtly Jewish about him, and we discover at the end that he is a vestigial Jew. This novel too, like his earlier ones, deals basically with the Jewish theme of redemptive suffering, and indicates Malamud's concern with the problem of adjustment of the modern Jew in America.

In Levin, Malamud deals with the experience of contemporary America in general, while he still retains the essentially Jewish attitudes. In his portrayal of the fumbling English instructor, the writer is close to the fact that the plight of the American Jew has lost its uniqueness, that condition of alienation is almost universal. Though Levin's Jewishness is no more than suggested, his quest for selfhood through love and experience are Jewish themes with American overtones, they are features of contemporary American life. In passing from Frank Alpine to S. Levin, Malamud has passed from describing the American as a Jew to describing the Jew as American. It can be said that in Levin the American and the Jew confront each other. Malamud's portrayal of Levin, blundering and progressing towards his objective, is a fictional demonstration of the declaration of one of his characters: 'There are Jews everywhere.'

In this novel, Malamud emerges from "the private world of fantasy with the larger world of academia."[46] But Levin, like

Roy and Frank, is in search of identity on social and emotional plans, though the two strands are closely intertwined, and are difficult to disentangle. On the social level, he seeks to establish himself as a teacher at Cascadia college, and on the emotional level, he seeks love. In a way, "*A New Life* continues the examination of the apprentice theme present in *The Assistant*. The earlier book described the conversion of Frank Alpine to the search for the good life, whereas in the latter the conversion has already taken place and the subject is the difficult conduct of the search."[47] However, "Seymour Levin, 'formerly a drunkard,' progresses—not like Frank Alpine from evil to good but from weakness and fear to strength and courage. An instructor at an agriculture college, Levin fumbles his way through teaching and into understanding."[48]

Like all Malamud's heroes, we find Levin at the beginning of the novel, on a journey from his past into the present—leaving behind, hopefully, "his weaknesses, impoverishment, indiscipline—the limp self entangled in the fabric of a will-less life."[49] In Malamud's fiction, journey is the symbol of quest and renewal. Frank had travelled to the east in search of better opportunities. Levin goes west "seeking, you might say, my manifest destiny" (108). In the past Levin's life has been full of failure and frustrations but in a moment of self-analysis he has 'a triumphant insight' into himself and realizes that he is made for a better destiny. Levin, like Frank, realizes he is a man of principles but does not know how to put them into practice.

On the personal front, although Levin has put his drunkenness behind him and has "awakened in his hole in the ground to a sense of life's holiness, he has not yet awakened to the love which makes those principles an actuality."[50] His experiences give him ample pain and unhappiness:

> Just when I thought I had discovered what would save me—when I believed it—my senses seemed to die, as though self-redemption wasn't possible because of what I was—my emptiness the sign of my worth . . . as a person I was nothing. (177)

It is this sense of nothingness or non-being which leads to his quest for "order, value, accomplishment and love" (189) in life.

It is when he will acquire meaning in life by acting responsibly that the feeling of non-being will be replaced by a sense of purpose.

It is his involvement with Pauline Gilley which leads to Levin's change of attitude towards others. From a selfish irresponsible person, Levin grows to be totally responsible and self-sacrificing. Initially, however, Levin's relationship with Pauline is also based on carnal desires. Engrossed in the fulfilment of his selfish demands, Levin refuses to reciprocate the love offered to him by Pauline. In Malamud's fiction, denial of love naturally brings pain, and with this painful experience begins Levin's initiation into the hard facts of reality—a painful process for Levin and an occasion of laughter for the readers. He continues to commit blunders and suffers from them till he learns to 'give' to others selflessly.

Levin cannot vivify the Cascading wasteland by his humanistic approach. He is not able to break through the conservative, conformist society of Cascadia. But Levin's act of submission to Pauline's demand that he renounces his college career in lieu of being allowed to keep the two children, subtracts from the affirmation he makes when he agrees to marry Pauline and accepts all her responsibilities too.

Levin is a *schlemiel* of the Jewish folklore tradition—"the ill-starred blunderer who can expect the worst return for the best intentions, evil for every kindness, punishment for every misdeed. For him to sin is to get caught. And Levin quickly proceeds to do both."[51] His is a typical Jewish fate, "for every pleasure, pain" (213). One sees, "the Jewish 'suffering' in Levin's final predicament—the moral assumption of the burdensome Pauline,"[52] when we hear Pauline relate how Levin was 'chosen' for nomination at the college. Pauline discloses that she "had picked out his photograph from among the rejected applicants and persuaded Gerald Gilley to give him job because his picture reminded me of a Jewish boy I have known in college who was very kind to me during a trying time in my life" (361). Levin thus realizes that he has been predestined to enact the role he thinks he chooses out of his free will.

*The Fixer* occupies a special place among Malamud's novels. In an interview, Malamud asserted:

> I wanted to write a book giving value to the human being . . . that's particularly important in times like these, when man seems almost in the course of being devalued. In many ways, you know, we are becoming a race of automatons—a race in which values other than human are considered the most important. This is a tendency I can feel in the air, and one that I wanted to oppose . . . that is my strongest book so far.[53]

The moral development of man that we saw in the earlier novels gains maturity in *The Fixer*. This novel images the physical and spiritual history of a Jew terribly caught up in Tsarist anti-Semitism. It presents the ordeal of the protagonist, Yakov Bok, a poor Jewish handyman, falsely accused of the ritual murder of a Christian child.

In *The Fixer*, the dramatic concern of Malamud is not to relate the details of Yakov's physical suffering for two and a half years in prison but to trace the process of moral growth in Yakov as engendered by his condition. Yakov undergoes intense physical and mental torture and in the process learns to be spiritually free though physically imprisoned. Malamud has said that his typical protagonist "is someone who fears his fate, is caught up in it,"[54] yet manages to outrun it. Thus, we witness "the crisis of moral consciousness in a pariah who has been forced to think for himself. He is forced out of animal cunning, out of the whimper of the animal to become little by little, a man."[55]

The theme of injustice and oppression which underlines the entire novel owes its origins to Malamud's unhappy awareness of the increasing persecution of the minorities by those who hypocritically process to uphold equality and justice. Malamud tells, "after my first novel, I was sniffing for an idea in the direction of injustice on the American scene. . . . I became involved with the theme in a way that set off my imagination in terms of art."[56] Within this novel, one of the characters, Bibikov, observes that society "has not changed in its essentials . . . even though we tend loosely to think of civilization as progress" and "there's something cursed . . . about a country where men have owned men as property."[57] Such thoughts attest to Malamud's despair at the increasing hatred among fellow beings and atrocities committed in the name of faith.

Like all Malamud's earlier heroes, we meet Yakov first when he is about to leave the *Shtetl* in search of a new life in Kiev. He begins, as every other protagonist does, with arrogance and self-centredness, yet lost, an orphan who feels that his life so far has been wasted and his opportunities in the *Shtetl* non-existent. Dissatisfied with the limitation of opportunities and possibilities in the confines of the *Shtetl*, Yakov breaks out in quest of better prospects abroad. He is a man full of wants, he feels, he will never satisfy in the *Shtetl*. "He is sick of living a life of impoverishment and frustration, and in Kiev he hopes to make a better living than he has in the past. . . . A job that pays roubles not noodles. Even some education" (15), he thinks. Through the image of Yakov leaving the *Shtetl* in quest of education and opportunity, Malamud dramatizes the contemporary man's urge to explore his self and affirm his identity.

Yakov Bok of *The Fixer* is a Jew without faith. He enters the novel as a free thinker. Though he had been religious when he was young he tells Bibikov that he had lost his belief in God: "What do I get from him but a bang on the head and a stream of piss in my face. So what is there to be worshipful about" (19), he tells his father-in-law, Samuel. Nowhere do in the novel does he find sustenance in the Jewish religion. In his terrible cell, "He thought of himself pursuing his enemies with God at his side, but when he looked at God all he saw or heard was a loud Ha Ha. It was his own imprisoned laughter" (189). His pious father-in-law, Shmuel, pleads with him to have faith in God reminding him that Job had said, "though he slay me, yet will I trust in him." But Yakov cries angrily:

> To win a lousy bet with the devil he killed off all the servants and innocent children of Job. For that alone I hate him, not to mention ten thousand pogroms. Ach, why do you make me talk fairy tales? Job is an invention and so is God. (232)

But despite his freethinking, Yakov Bok, is still a Jew. Though he tries to deny his Jewish identity, he finds that he cannot—events force it upon him. Bok cannot escape his Jewishness by dropping his bag of prayer things into the Dneiper from fear of an anti-Semitic boatman, or by assuming a Russian name and a false identity as an overseer. His false position makes him uncomfortable, "something that unexpectedly bothered him was that he was no longer using his tools" (59). Bok's innate Jewishness sometimes shows itself unexpectedly. On one occasion he follows Zina to her bedroom and finds that she is 'unclean.' Bok will not touch her, he will not violate the Law. Even when Yakov rescues the old Jew, Hasid, his deep-seated Jewishness becomes evident because he accepts the commitment to be human, which is the essence of Jewishness. It is, therefore, grimly appropriate that as the essential Jew, he should be made the conscience-keeper of the Kiev Jewry and be charged with the murder of the Christian boy. Behind the fixer's arrest, there is a complex set of circumstances that is not immediately apparent.

Yakov's problem is the typical problem of all heroes of Malamud: the urge to stand alone from society and affirm the unique self in isolation from the rest of the world, outside history. The enforced incarceration of Yakov gives him ample opportunity to meditate on his predicament and realize his futility of attempting to evade commitments in this world and achieve authenticity in isolation. The fixer's interior journey into his self begins with his predicament of the disparity between the private image of himself and the mask of the fanatical Jew sought to be thrust on him by the anti-Semites of Kiev. His certainties regarding his past and his place in society are shaken up, and in the hatred that is directed against him, he finds that his true self is invisible. He might ask himself: "Christ. Despite his disavowal of Judaism, the people of Kiev regard him a blood drinking-monster; a repository of primitive inhuman forces" (152).

Yakov hopes at first that it is only a question of mistaken identity, and thinks that "if he only explained why he had done what he had done, he would at once be released" (68). But the fact of his innocence is not perceived by the gentiles, who consider him a murderous Jew. Yakov's progress consists in his involvement towards being the representative Jew—bridging the gap between his private vision of himself and the image society has of him.

The fixer gradually progresses from living in a moral vacuum without an authentic code of values, to manhood, evolving in the process a code of values tested and verified by his experience. In the prison he is driven more and more into himself as his freedom is gradually reduced to the point of non-existence. His isolation as a human being is seen in his contempt for the Russians. In a way his imprisonment is a necessary stage in his progress towards acceptance of pain and suffering as the medium of human existence. As Robert Alter writes: "The prison . . . is Malamud's way of suggesting that to be fully a man is to accept the most painful limitations; those who escape these limitations achieve an illusory, self-negating kind of freedom, for they become less than responsible human beings."[58]

But a positive indication of the direction of the fixer's quest is provided by his preoccupation with the philosophy of Spinoza, who like Yakov, had been "out to make a freeman of himself" (71). It is Spinoza who had helped Yakov develop his new spiritual freedom. Yakov confesses, "when I was reading Spinoza I stayed up night after night. I was by now excited by ideas and I tried to collect a few of my own. It was the beginning of a different Yakov" (192). The different Yakov is the one who grows in maturity to the extent that he can transcend the reality of his imprisonment. He had said to Raisel: "Don't be superstitious. . . . If you want to be free, first be free in your mind" (191). It is only after he gains maturity that he applies this idea for his own good. This is what Yakov learns—to be a free man he must seek inner freedom, freedom from self. Yakov also learns that the purpose of freedom is to create it for others. Bibikov urges Yakov not to "withdraw from the task if he has some small thing to offer, for if he does so it will be at "the risk of diminishing his humanity" (157). Thus, what we trace in *The Fixer* is "the imprisonment of Yakov Bok's psychological and moral self . . . and his gradual emergence from that spiritual confinement."[59]

With spiritual freedom comes objectivity. He learns to view his experience dispassionately and rationally. He accepts the irrational forces of the world, "the world was the kind it was. The rain put out fires and caused floods. Yet too much happened that didn't make sense. . . . Things go badly at a historical moment and go that way, God or no God, forever" (139-40). Yakov finds consolation in Ostrovsky's words that "those who persecute the innocent were themselves never free" (282). His attitude towards his Russian persecutors also changes; while at first he had raged in hate against them, he now says, "the truth of it is in his heart no one's enemy but his own" (246). By the end, he is mature enough to reflect, "it had happened—he was back to this again—because he was Yakov Bok and has learned, it was not easy . . . still, it was better than not knowing. A man had to learn, it was his nature" (282-83).

Yakov succeeds where Levin had failed. Levin, unable to compromise his social responsibilities, had failed in his role of teacher as liberator. Yakov, on the other hand, had given top priority to his social role as a redeemer of his downtrodden race and has succeeded in living up to his role. Yakov also succeeds in fulfilling his responsibilities in his personal life and is thus morally the most victorious of Malamud's heroes.

In *The Tenants*, Malamud holds the conviction that humanism is possible not only despite the antinomies but even because of them. Denil Stern defines the basic theme in Malamud's novels driven by "one's sense of values it's a vision in imaginary world."[60] The informing motive in Malamud's works is the necessity of accommodation in this world. In fact, 'morality' is nothing but a mode of accommodation. Malamud's characters live in a world of interpersonal relationships and as per Malamud's norms the hero needs to realize and fulfil obligations to others. The inspiring factor to create *The Tenants*, Malamud tells us was, "Jew and Blacks, the period of the troubles in the New York City," and, "All I know is that American blacks have been badly treated. We, as a society, have to redress the balance."[61]

Malamud again and again stresses on the necessity of accommodation, "we must accept limits on one's needs in order to live effectively with others, so that the gift of life may function."[62]

Harry Lesser, a Jewish writer, the protagonist of *The Tenants* is an isolated individual living in a prison of his own making. Like Morris Bober was in the store, Lesser lives entombed in the tenement. He does not feel the need to communicate with the world around him. Inevitably, Lesser appears to be moving towards the act of cutting himself off from life. However, by Malamud's code of morality, "Goodness is achieved not in a vacuum, but in the company of other man, attended by love."[63] Hence, Lesser must transcend himself and burst his prison to relate to others. He must lose the sense of being set apart and sympathize with others. He must feel a sense of community.

Lesser has been creating a novel for a decade and for which he can find no end. He tries to convince his landlord, that his novel, if he can bring it to a conclusion, will help Levenspiel to "understand and endure"[64] his own life. Levenspiel protests, "what's a make-believe novel, Lesser, against all my woes and miseries that I have explained to you?" (22). For Levenspiel, life outweighs art. Regarding Lesser's talk of art he comments: "Art my ass, in this world it's heart that counts" (23). However, Lesser finds it impossible to combine 'life' and 'art.'

Lesser fails to understand the futility of art as a sphere unconnected with the actualities of life. Art is inclined towards morality, Malamud has often said, only Lesser does not understand it. Malamud has asserted: "Morality begins with an awareness of the sanctity of life, hence the lives of others. Art, in essence, celebrates life and gives us our measure."[65] Ihab Hassan touches the core of the problem in *The Tenants* when he states, "Art can still take and give the human measure of things though artists themselves may be obstructed."[66]

Lesser's cocooned lifestyle gets wrecked by Willie Spearmint, a writer aspirant who comes to shake Lesser's empty tenement. Their common passion—writing—brings them together. Lesser sees in Willie a "fellow writer [who] may be future friend" (38). In this relationship of black untutored writer apprenticed to the white experienced writer, Malamud characterized his favourite motif of the double—two characters whose destinies are linked in various ways. When Lesser steals Irene's love from Willie that later ends his apprenticeship to Lesser and asserts his freedom by changing his name from Willie Spearmint to Bill Spear. As a black he denies that anyone but a black can understand the black predicament; only a black can know what it is to suffer for being black: "This is a black book we are talking about you don't understand at all. White fiction ain't the same as black. It can't be" (60). He asserts, "you want to know what's really art? I am art. Willie Spearmint, Blackman. My form is myself" (61). He becomes an emblem of the black community.

Lesser and Willie hate each other yet need each other and most of all suffer together. The two are linked not only by their mutual hatred and fear but by their common struggle as writers also. As Lesser and Willie fight, the victim and the assailant become confused as one person. The relationship of enemy to enemy and of accusation to guilt is hard to distinguish. Leslie Field says, "The tangled motive of shared guilt and victim, and victimizer prove equally culpable,"[67] become central to the relationship between Lesser and Willie.

Malamud does not mitigate the terrible actuality of racial acrimony by offering an optimistic ending. The inter-racial miracles are invalid in the grim world of today. He asserts that *The Tenants* "is a sort of prophetic warning against fanaticism," and it "argues for the invention of choices to outwit tragedy. It is these choices which keep the possibility of racial reconciliation open and yet distrust any easy solution."[68] *The Tenants*, Ihab Hassan comments, "is true both to its author's vision and to his sense of the altered times."[69] Malamud's vision is not nihilistic nor has he radically revised his stand regarding the importance of basic values in man's life. He maintains his integrity of moral purpose. The focus on the stark reality of racial hatred and insensate violence is part of the process of establishing his values. He hopes to shock the reader into an awareness of the absurdity of reality caused by disavowal of love. Such objective of reality becomes the very source of the validity of Malamud's premises.

The purpose of the novel, *Dubin's Lives*, is evaluation of self, "What had my experience totaled up to? What did I know upto this point? I wanted to write a novel that was significant to me."[70] In comparison to his earlier works, Malamud said, "the texture of it, the depth of it, the quality of human experience in it is greater than my previous books."[71] All of Malamud's earlier novels spoke of moral possibilities of man through purgative suffering and selfless love. Malamud's later novels, however, fall outside the sphere of suffering and moral accountability which forms the basis of his earlier novels.

The undercurrent of pessimism that ran throughout *The Tenants* is there in *Dubin's Lives* also. Critics conclude that the "discrepancies between the emotional tenor of his books and their instructional promises have become too extreme for patching up and have threatened to fracture the Malamudian universe altogether."[72] However, a closer study of the novel reveals that though Malamud does reject his often repeated moral conservatism, his protagonist William B. Dubin, a biographer, is made to learn through his experience; no moral injunctions are imposed upon him. Though Malamud has not let Dubin's experiences come under the dictates of any moral patterns yet one may draw, at times, moral inferences from the outcome of the experiences. There is nothing fabulistic about *Dubin's Lives*. In it Malamud proves himself "a realist in the sense Dostoevsky was, a writer true to the structures of experience."[73] Unlike Malamud's earlier heroes, Dubin seeks no redemption, though, like the others, he does seek a new life and acceptance.

Dubin, the protagonist, is the new activist hero. He seeks escape from the stagnation of his everyday existence and for a personally meaningful identity. When we first meet him, his real concern is for his life in totality. Dubin is like all activist heroes who are "wholly concerned with their own special private irritations, their own erotic needs, anxious, frantic as to the meaning for themselves alone in their adventure in love."[74] He is restless to experience some events "against which he can exercise fully and satisfactorily a personal sense of will, of agency."[75]

Dubin recalls his childhood as a son of a poor Jewish waiter, but the orthodoxy of his parents has made no imprint on him. When he decides to marry Kitty, his father says miserably: "why do you want to marry a boyish child that he will someday call you names. . . . You know what we went through with Hitler. Don't marry somebody that will take you away from the Jewish people"[76] and Dubin replies: "Dear Papa, how can a man be a Jew if he isn't a man? How can he be a man if he gives up the woman he wants to marry?" (81). Daniel Fuchs looks at the complexity of this dilemma:

> The question then arises: how much of a Jew is Dubin? He is not observant, marries a non-Jew, does not maintain a Jewish household, and rarely talks to his children about Jewish. His most explicit statement about Jewishness is negative. He defends his marrying a Shiksa to his old father. . . . The question of conversion never comes up for Dubin. He is an ethical Jew, whose ethics include discarding what is identifiably Jewish when it matters. In a sense Dubin's relation to Jewishness parallels Malamud's to his earlier 'Jewish' writing—something he wanted to outgrow.[77]

Dubin suffers, one does not feel that he suffers as a victim or that suffering is his fate because he is a Jew. Unlike Malamud's earlier characters who were gentle Jewish martyrs like Morris Bobar, Dubin, though born a Jew and now only marginally so, is no martyr. Indeed, it is his Catholic wife, Kitty, who suffers as a victim of Dubin's own psychological upheavals and its effects on their marriage. In his indecisiveness, Dubin will not give up one for the other and as a result both Kitty and Fanny suffer. Kitty, because of his growing intolerance towards "her sameness, dissatisfactions, eccentricities; he was bored with her fears, her unforgotten past" (269), and Fanny because of his non-committal attitude towards her. Dubin himself suffers most from his indecisiveness and comes to the conclusion, "life is forever fleeting, our fates juggled heartbreakingly by events we can't foresee or control and we are always pitifully vulnerable to what happens next" (42).

Nor can one limit Dubin's experience to the confines of the Jewish plight and existential plight: the suffering and the utter loneliness characterizing the Jew's experience for two thousand years becomes in modern times, everyone's condition and offers the Jew as a symbol of the modern predicament. Fredrick J. Hoffman offers a similar observation but one that emphasizes the self-assertion rather than the victimization of the hero, "The Jewish situation is an existential one, within limits. The self-assertion in this circumstance, is hedged by doubts, by a comic self-consciousness but ultimately the hero's decision is all but entirely his own; he has a tradition, but it demands that he acts on his own initiative."[78] In *Dubin's Lives*, "there is a Jewish quality that persists. For better or worse Jewishness is defined by Dubin as a sense of obligation, a way of doing things characterized by the restraints of decency."[79] He can transcend the universal chaos by way of compassion and moral commitment.

Malamud has written about man's struggle against destructive forces before. In *The Assistant*, Morris Bober, the grocer, struggles against crushing poverty; in *The Fixer*, Yakov Bok struggles against the forces of anti-Semitism that try to destroy his freedom and his will; and in *The Tenants*, the white writer Harry Lesser struggles against habits of racism when he tries to be friends with the black writer Willie Spearmint.

But in *God's Grace*, the destructive force is the most absolute of all—nuclear war—and Malamud's conclusion the bleakest of all—utter devastation. God, however, overlooked one man Calvin Cohn, a Jewish paleologist who was poking around at bottom of the sea in an oceanography vessel, Rebekah Q, when the bombs blew between the Djanks and the Druzhkies. As God explains to him, "I made man free, but his freedom, badly used, destroyed him."[80] Malamud asserted, "The question of man's freedom has always interested me. How much of the freedom does he has? How far does it extend? And ultimately, what does he do with it? It's the last part that bothers me most. I'm not going to gainsay man's accomplishments, but I still feel there's a vast sense of failure that has clouded his best efforts to produce a greater freedom than he was born with."[81]

Cohn broods over his fate as the lone survivor of all humanity. He tries to figure out God's inscrutable purpose in letting him live. He wonders if he has been chosen by God to recreate life on earth. God speaks to him through a crack in the sky and dispels all wishful thinking. Cohn, he states, escaped destruction because through a minuscule error—a minor slip-up in the cosmic plan, therefore, he must not have any false expectations. It is an oversight God will shortly rectify: "I must slay you, it is just. Yet because of my error, I will grant you time to compose yourself, make your peace. Therefore live quickly—a few deep breaths and go your way" (13). Cohn begs to be allowed to live. "He who saves one life, it is as if he saved the world" (13), he quotes from the Sanhedrin. However, God is angry and will not revoke His orders; He will make "no exceptions, righteous or otherwise" (13).

Cohn rants, Job-like, against God for letting man destroy himself and for causing the flood to engulf the earth again. "God counts, man has failed Him; he has not proved himself worthy of His grace . . . they have destroyed my handiwork, the conditions of their survival," God states (12). Man's lack of self-control and his violent nature has brought upon him self-annihilation. Thus, humanity has done itself in; only God looked away and let the world burn in the scorching nuclear holocaust. Cohn mourns for "human being, human existence, goodness, daring, joy; and all that man has done well" (17). In rage and in grief, Cohn contends with the wrathful God for destroying His own dream, "Why hadn't he created man equal to whom He had imagined?" Cohn demands (126). God asserts that He made man imperfect so that he may strive to perfect himself. God withdraws his presence and snaps the crack shut in the cloud.

Cohn feels abandoned and desolate on the battered vessel. Soon, however, he discovers a young chimpanzee, Buz. Cohn impatiently speaks to Buz:

> The situation is getting on my nerves. I mean we're alone on this island and can't be said to speak to each other. We may indicate certain things but there is no direct personal communication. I'm not referring to existential loneliness, you understand—what might be called awareness of one's subjective being, not without some sense of death-in-life, if you know what I mean. I'm talking,

> rather, about the loneliness one feels when he lacks companionship, or that sense of company that derives from community. (53)

Cohn finds the realm of possibility expand with his discovery of an experimental chimpanzee who had not only been trained but has also been converted to Christianity. Cohn adopts the chimpanzee, Buz, as a son and changes his name from the German sounding Gottlob ('God-praise') to the Jewish Buz after "One of the descendants of Nahor, the brother of Abraham the Patriarch, therefore, a name of sterling worth" (27). Encouraged by his discovery of another living being, the Malamud protagonist, once again, sets about to create a new life for himself as his past life has come to nothing.

Like many of Malamud's heroes, Cohn is a lapsed Jew. He had changed his first name, from 'Seymour' his father gave him to Calvin, perhaps more than coincidentally the name of the Protestant reformer. Cohn had also given up his rabbinic studies to become a paleontologist because he was always interested in the beginnings of things. His Judaism had slipped to little more than an interest in God as First Cause, but on his Island, Cohn wants to make better Jews of the chimps than himself. Cohn hopes to establish functioning social community based on "a higher order of behaviour—to a former lower order of creatures" (119). He takes upon himself the role of advisor and teacher. He starts a school to educate the perceptive chimps. Cohn lectures the primates on ethics, religion, philosophy and the history of the civilization destroyed. He addresses them on a variety of topics and inspiring, discipline, mutuality and responsibility towards other chimps. He constantly talks to them of the sins man committed so that they may avoid repeating man's worst errors in the future society; "men had failed each other in obligations and responsibilities—failed to achieve brotherhood, lost their lovely worlds, not to mention living lives" (119).

Thus, Cohn makes all efforts to establish a society based on human ethics. The most noteworthy aspect of Cohn's teaching is that he draws his inspiration from the Jewish scriptures and traditions. Cohn alludes profusely to the ethical teachings of the

Pentateuch and the Hebrew scriptures in teaching his 'fellow' primates. He sets up the Seven Admonitions, "which reflect a cautiously hopeful, pragmatic view of the necessity for altruism and of man's small but real potential for good."[82] Overtly, *God's Grace* is the most Jewish of all the novels of Malamud. "Cohn is vulnerable, comic, earthly, ironic. . . . His Jewishness is playful and serious, secular and spiritual, repository of family memory and a measure of morality,"[83] opines Alan Lelchuck.

II

Malamud's first collection of short stories *The Magic Barrel*, "captures the poetry of human relations at a point where imagination and reality meet."[84] Though it is possible to classify the stories as those pertaining to Jews and non-Jews of New York, and some pertaining to the Italian background, but this collection as a whole tends to be "an affirmation of man's ability to realize himself, even in the face of deprivation and disaspter."[85] *The Magic Barrel* contains thirteen stories, and the first one, "The First Seven Years" indicates that Malamud is interested in developing the possibilities of an apprentice character with a view to commenting on the value of possibility, hope and dedication to an ideal. Besides being a realistic portrayal of the hardships of the Immigrant Jews in America, this story is equally concerned with the mysteries of human heart. In "The Mourners," the problems of poverty and social responsibility recur more insistently. Kessler had abandoned his wife and children, but the guilt of desertion does not let him live in peace. In "Angel Levine," Malamud seems to be conscious of the complex pattern of relationship between Jews and Blacks that he has exhibited in *The Tenants*. In "The Lady of the Lake," the quality of personal integrity is tested. The drama of compassion and concern is central to "Take Pity." In the same way, "The Prison" depicts the manner in which "the soul descends into an embitteringly nightmare when the need to expand goodness is denied."[86] The story "The Magic Barrel" is concerned with the selection of a bride for Leo Finkel. It is this vision of human survival in the stories of Malamud that Kazin admires:

> And it does seem to me that the tangibility, the felt reverberations of life that one finds in a writer like Bernard Malamud, spring from his belief that any imaginative world, no matter how local or strange is the world, and that for the imaginative writer values must be considered truths not subjective fancies. It is really a kind of faith that accounts for Malamud's 'perfect sympathy' with his characters in *The Assistant* and *The Magic Barrel*. Though it is difficult to sympathize with each other, it is a fact that fiction elicit and prove the world we share, that it can display the unforeseen possibilities of the human—even when everything seems dead set against it.[87]

*Idiots First* is a collection of eleven stories and one dramatic sketch. Out of these twelve pieces "Still Life" and "Naked Nude" dealing with Fidelman and Italian locale were later included in *Pictures of Fidelman*. In these tales of Jews both hapless and affluent, Malamud's intention is not to Judaize society but to suggest the possibility of humanizing it. Malamud says, "All men are Jews . . . although few men know it."[88] The shaping impulse behind this statement is Malamud's anxiety to highlight common human response to suffering, for instance, which tends to obliterate the outer differences among different people. In a review of the stories, Bellman observes: "Malamud's compelling force as one of our major talents comes from his ability to evoke the sense that he identifies his Jews as modern everymen."[89] The first story 'Idiots First' deals with Mendel and his idiot son, Issac. It is an impressive account of the destitution as well as commitment to the value of love. "Black is My Favourite Color" expresses the racial problem between black and Jews in a forthright manner. Hoyt calls it "an interesting new variation of Malamud's theme, a poignant account of the overwhelming difficulties in the way of honest relationships between different races."[90] In "The Death of Me," Malamud takes up the problem of communication between two persons of the same religious community, what Malamud seems to convey is that the deadlock in human relationships is not always because of different racial attitudes but also because of opposing individual oddities of temper. Instead of being parochial towards Jews, Malamud handles them as severely as he would treat the non-Jews. It is the withering away of compassionate understanding of one another that ruins the possibility of a dialogue in life.

The story "The Jewbird" deals allegorically with the theme of anti-Semitism. A bedraggled black Jewbird named Schwartz enters through an open window of Harry Cohen's apartment near the Lower East River. Pursued by anti-Semite he seeks protection in the home of a fellow-Jew who is, however, allergic to his foul smell. However, it is the last story, "The German Refugee," that deals with Oskar Gassner, who flees the Nazis and comes to America which exposes the horror of anti-Semitism that have been suggested in "The Jewbird." The story "The German Refugee" tends to delineate the magnitude of racial insanity and its social and moral ramifications.

In all these stories Malamud seems to be concerned with the problem of comprehension in life. By relenting the opportunity to understand fellow-beings, men embitter their lives through an idiotic pursuit of narrow-self interest. In their persistence to remain morally impervious, they "cannot connect with one another."[91] By pointing out human flaw Malamud seeks to project his admiration for those who know to suffer for others. It is Malamud's defence of humanity that Ratner notices in these stories:

> However, the permanent value in Malamud lies in his poetic sensibility to the implications of his stories and his belief in a moral humanistic code of behaviour, a belief in real, not abstract, commitment. The modern concern for a man of flesh and bone, basically absurd and tragic at the same time, is distinctly relevant to Malamud's fiction; often all that he portrays of man's condition is his situation but his work ultimately affirms his being that through self-scrutiny, suffering, and sympathy men can recreate their humanity.[92]

While it renders the dilemmas and aspirations of man, *Idiots First* tends to exemplify Malamud's defence of the human territory.

The collection *Pictures of Fidelman* is an episodic novel written by Malamud over a period of twelve years. All the stories deal with the misadventures of Fidelman who comes to Europe in quest of his vocation, and in search of love and each successive story 'grows' in his awareness of life and art. Malamud's goal in these stories is to have his comic hero, "find himself both in art and self-knowledge."[93] Fidelman, the 'faithful' does so, but he also discovers that both art and self are quite different from what he thought them to be. As is always in Malamud's fiction, Fidelman has to move towards salvation through various archetypal ordeals and humiliations. Once again the thematic core is "the search for romance, in life and in the stories of European art, and the discovery of reality of the quester's own true nature and condition."[94] The exhibition is of a "panel of pictures reminiscent of Hogarth" which sets forth Fidelman's progress "down and out of salvation."[95]

In the first story "Last Mohican," having failed as a painter, Fidelman like Frank Alpine decides to change his life. Like S. Levin, who goes west in quest of a new life, he turns to art history and comes to Italy. He is full of aspirations and eager to begin some form of new life. But being a quintessence Malamud hero, he seeks something for himself and is yet excessively protective of his own interests, but it is not long before he finds that he like all Malamud's heroes, is caught in "a compromised environment which offers a wide variety of the frustrations to their particular aspirations . . . and one of the effects of their sufferings in the compromised environment is to then redefine the form and content of that notional new life."[96]

Fidelman, the irrepressible Malamud *Schlemiel*, attracts troubles right upon his arrival in the form of Shimon Susskind, a *schnorrer* (artful beggar), who starts right away to pester him for charity. Not satisfied with the couple of notes the pedantic art critic reluctantly gives him, Susskind demands a suit. Fidelman, however, repudiates any demands made on him. He reorganizes his routine to avoid Susskind and devotes himself solely to the study of Giotto. Unconscious of his own ancient heritage he marvels and gushes over all the Roman history around him in Italy. "It was an inspiring business, he, Arthur Fidelman, after all born a Bronx boy, walking around in all this history."[97] And amidst such history this modern Wandering Jew seeks a new understanding of himself and a better fate.

The collection *Rambrandt's Hat* consists of eight short stories. These stories, by no means short, are neither wholly cheerful nor totally depressing but a mixed fare like most of the human situations. In the first story "The Silver Crown" Albert seeks faith healing for his father who is in the hospital with heart cancer. It is difficult to ascertain the thematic thrust in the story juxtaposing the words of uncritical faith and pervasive rationality. Avoiding sentimentality Malamud seeks to portray the tender ties between the father and son. The values of his relationship, however, can be appreciated not through Albert's momentary gush of emotion but through his critical reaction to his father's attitude. Restoring to a supernatural aid does not alleviate the pain of life, and it is to suffer this pain that Albert revokes his alliance with the Rabbi.

"The Man in the Drawer" is the longest story in the book. The concern of man for man is the shaping impulse of the story. The themes in Feliks's stories are the ones that centralize Malamud's creative vision. Even when Feliks chooses to write about the Russian Jews, the animating impulse seems to be to draw on his area of experience. Since he is a 'marginal Jew' and an 'atheist,' as he tells Howard, his choice of Jewish characters should not be interpreted as an instance of ethnic preference. It is the ethnic slant in Stern's reaction to Feliks's stories that sounds a bit prescriptive. Referring to these pieces, Stern remarks: "In them people who are not Jewish in any religious or traditional sense involve themselves with Jewishness as an act of identification with Jews who are bring punished for their identity. Jewishness is a road to authenticity."[98]

*Rembrandt's Hat*, like 'pictures' of Fidelman, deals with the complex problem of human relationship, for it is related to Malamud's ultimate vision of life which takes into cognizance the obsessions and incongruities of human temperaments. It is worth remembering that Malamud is not oblivious of the limitations of self while projecting his protagonist's search for acceptance and authenticity. Malamud is actually conscious of the polarities of human freedom and necessity.

Malamud's protagonist seeks connection with the world, but in failing to attain connection with his own nature, he finds that the world to which he fits his face turns into a chaos of unfulfilment. Malamud's Jews do possess an ancient identity and that they bear it consciously or unconsciously. The next chapter deals with the struggle to establish unity with some unacknowledged centre of the protagonist's personality, that is to say, a struggle to unite with lost roots.

## NOTES

1. Charles Angoff, and Meyer Levin, ed., "Introduction," *The Rise of Jewish American Literature* (New York: Simon and Schuster, 1970) 7.
2. Sheldon Norman Grebstain, "Bernard Malamud and the Jewish Movement," Leslie A. Field and Joyce W. Field, ed., *Bernard Malamud: A Collection of Critical Essays* (Twentieth Century Views; New Jersey: Prentice-Hall, 1975) 18.
3. Max F. Schulz, *Radical Sophistication: Studies in Contemporary Jewish-American Novelists* (Athens, Ohio: Ohio Univ. Press, 1969) 3.
4. Leslie A. Fiedler, "The Jew as Mythic American," *Ramparts*, 2 (1963) 32.
5. Robert Alter, "Jewish Dreams and Nightmares," Irving Malin, ed. *Contemporary American-Jewish Literature: Critical Essays* (Bloomington: Indiana Univ. Press, 1973) 59.
6. Irving Malin, *Jews and Americans* (Carbondale: Southern Illinois Press, 1965) 10.
7. *Ibid.*
8. *Ibid.*
9. Paul Luther, "The Jewish Hero: Two Views," *The New Republic* (November 24, 1958) 18.
10. Ernest Van Den Haag, *The Jewish Mystique* (New York: Delta, 1971) 33.
11. Qtd. Bernard Cohen, *Socio-Cultural Changes in American-Jewish Life: As Reflected in Selected Jewish Literature* (Rutherford: Fairleigh Dickinson Univ. Press, 1972) 28.

12. *Ibid.*, 22.
13. Ernest Van Den Haag, 53.
14. *Ibid.*, 87.
15. Bernard Cohen, 226.
16. *Ibid.*, 240.
17. Irving Malin, 228.
18. Emanuel Feldman, "The American and Jew," Norman Lammand Walter and S. Wursburger, ed., *A Treasury of Tradition* (New York: Hebrew Publishing, 1967) 138.
19. *Ibid.*
20. Irving Malin, 59.
21. Abraham Josua Heschel, "God in Search of Man," Irving Malin, ed., *Jews and American*, 58.
22. Harold Laski, *The American Dream* (New York: Viking Press, 1948) 76.
23. *Ibid.*, 143.
24. *Ibid.*, 144.
25. Ihab Hassan, *Contemporary American Literature 1945-1972* (New York: Frederick Unger, 1973) 71.
26. *Ibid.*, 72.
27. Max F. Schulz, 6.
28. *Ibid.*, 5.
29. Robert Alter, 71.
30. Philip Roth, *Reading Myself and Others* (New York: Farrar, Straus and Giroux, 1975) 127.
31. Granville Hicks, *Literary Horizons: A Quarter Century of American Fiction* (New York: New York Press, 1970) 219.
32. Sidney Richman, *Bernard Malamud* (New York: Twayne, 1966) 29.
33. Tony Tanner, *City of Words: American Fiction 1950-1970* (New York: Harper and Row, 1971) 323.
34. Bernard Malamud, *The Natural* (Harmondsworth: Penguin 1967) 30.
35. Leslie A. Field and Joyce W. Field, "An Interview with Bernard Malamud," *Bernard Malamud: A Collection of Critical Essays*, 15.
36. Sidney Richman, 15.
37. Joseph Wershba, 7.
38. Qtd. Granville Hicks, "His Hope on the Human Heart," *Saturday Review* (October 12, 1963) 32.
39. Sidney Richman, 43.
40. *Ibid.*, 54.

41. Bernard Malamud, *The Assistant* (Harmondsworth: Penguin, 1967) 84.
42. Ben Siegal, "Victims in Motion: Bernard Malamud's Sad and Bitter Clowns," *North-West Review*, 5: 2 (1962) 70.
43. Jonathan Baumbach, "The Economy of Love: The Novels of Bernard Malamud," *Kenyon Review*, 25 (1963) 451.
44. *Ibid.*, 455.
45. Marcus Klein, *After Alienation: American Novel in Mid-Century* (New York: World Book Publishing, 1963) 260.
46. Samuel A. Weiss, "Passion and Purgation in Bernard Malamud," *Univ. of Windsor Review*, 2: 1 (1966) 98.
47. Granville Hicks, 32
48. Robert Scholas, "Portraits of Artist as 'Escape Goat,'" *Saturday Review*, 52 (1969) 33.
49. Bernard Malamud, *A New Life* (New York: Avon, 1980) 163.
50. Sidney Richman, 87.
51. Ben Siegal, 72.
52. Helen Weinberg, *The New Novel in America: The Kafkan Mode in Contemporary Fiction* (Ithaca: Cornell Univ. Press, 1970) 177.
53. Harold Hughes, "The Man Behind *The Fixer*," *The Oregonian* (1966) 21.
54. Israel Shenker, "The Malamud It's Story," *New York Times Book Review* (October 3, 1971) 23.
55. V.S. Pritchett, "A Pariah," *New York Review of Books* (September 22, 1966) 10.
56. Granville Hicks, "One Man to Stand for Six Million," *Saturday Review*, 49 (1966) 37.
57. Bernard Malamud. *The Fixer* (Harmondsworth: Penguin, 1967) 150.
58. Robert Alter, "Bernard Malamud: Jewishness as Metaphor," Leslie A. Field and Joyce W. Field, ed., *Bernard Malamud and the Critics* (New York: New York Univ. Press, 1970) 30.
59. William J. Handy, "The Malamud Hero: A Quest for Existence," Richard Astro and Jackson J. Benson, ed., *The Fiction of Bernard Malamud* (Cornvallis: Oregon State Univ. Press, 1977) 30.
60. Daniel Stern, "The Art of Fiction: Bernard Malamud," *The Paris Review*, 61 (1975) 65.
61. *Ibid.*, 61.
62. E.H.Leelavalthi Masilamoni, "Bernard Malamud—An Interview." *Indian Journal of American Studies*, 9 (1997) 33.

63. Saul Bellow, *Dangling Man* (New York: Penguin, 1944) 75.
64. Bernard Malamud, *The Tenants* (Harmondsworth: Penguin, 1971) 22.
65. Qtd. Ihab Hassan, "Bernard Malamud: 1976 Fictions within Our Fictions," Richard Astro and Jackson J. Benson, 43.
66. *Ibid.*, 46.
67. Ben Siegel, 139.
68. Israel Shanker, 22.
69. Ihab Hassan, 54.
70. Ralph Tyler, "A Talk with the Novelist," *New York Times Book Review* (February 18, 1979) 31.
71. *Ibid.*, 32.
72. Mark Shechner, "The Return of the Repressed," *The Nation*, 228 (1979) 227.
73. Richard Gilman, "Magic and Morality," *The New Republic* (March 24, 1979) 28.
74. David L. Stevenson, "The Activist" *Daedalus*, 92 (1963) 238.
75. *Ibid.*, 247.
76. Bernard Malamud, *Dubin's Lives* (Harmondsworth: Penguin, 1979) 280.
77. Daniel Fuchs, "Malamud's Dubin's Lives:.A Jewish Writer and the Sexual Ethic," *Studies in American-Jewish Literature*, 7: 2 (1998) 159.
78. Fredrick J. Hoffman, "Dogmatic Innocence: Self-Assertion in Modern American Literature," *Texas Quarterly*, 6 (1963) 159.
79. Daniel Fuchs, 208.
80. Bernard Malamud, *God's Grace* (Harmondsworth: Penguin, 1982) 13.
81. Helen Benedict, 29.
82. Robert Alter, "A Theological Fantasy," *The New Republic* (September 28, 1982) 39.
83. Alan Lelchuck, "Malamud's Dark Fable," *New York Times Book Review,* 87 (1982) 15.
84. Granville Hicks, 32.
85. *Ibid.*
86. Sidney Richman, 111.
87. Alfred Kazin, "The Alone Generation," Marcus Klein, *After Alienation*, 123.
88. Henry Popkin, "The Jewish Stories," *The Kenyan Review*, 20 (1963) 637.

89. Samuel Irving Bellman, "Women, Children and *Idiots First*: Transformation Psychology," Leslie A. Field and Joyce W. Field, 15.
90. Charlès Alva Hoyt, "The New Romanticism," Leslie A. Field and Joyce W. Field, 182.
91. Marc L. Ratner, "Style and Humanity in Malamud's Fiction," *Massachusetts Review*, 5: 4 (1964) 670.
92. *Ibid.*, 683.
93. Sale Roger, "What Went Wrong?" *New York Times Review of Books* (October 21, 1971) 6.
94. Christof Wegelin, "The American *Schlemiel* Abroad: Malamud's Italian Stories and the End of American Innocence," *Twentieth Century Literature*, 19 (1973) 80.
95. Robert Scholes, 33.
96. Tony Tanner, 322.
97. Bernard Malamud, *Pictures of Fidelman: An Exhibition* (Harmondsworth: Penguin, 1969) 16.
98. Daniel Stern, "Commonplace Things, and the Essence of Art," *The Nation* (September 3, 1973) 182.

# Lost Roots

In the post-second World War novel, the protagonist is involved in an interminable search through the cluster of everyday existence for sense of satisfying identity. Richard Lehan writes that the contemporary American novelists "Bellow, Wright, Ellison—all are concerned with the meaning of identity in the modern world, the nature of good and evil, the possibility of fulfilment in the contemporary society, the course of value in a world without God, and the possibility and meaning of action in an ethical vacuum."[1] In novel the central figure is a twentieth century 'isolato,' understandably preoccupied with preserving his individuality from the abstract constructs which categorize him into invisibility. He is always an alert and avid investigator, always on the lookout for change in experience and hopes for fresh perception.

Bernard Malamud's characters are characteristically reflective and introspective, each possessing the desire and an innate capacity for conscious awareness of his existence. Each character is confronted with the existential question "who am I?" rather than the metaphysical question "what am I?" Obviously, the protagonist confronts himself and a critical self-appraisal leads him ultimately to self-discovery. Lionel Trilling writes: "In its essence literature is concerned with self, and the particular concern of the literature of the past two centuries has been with self in its standing quarrel with culture."[2] The contemporary form of that quarrel has been bequeathed to the American Jew by nature of his history. The ability of the Jews to move beyond parochialism, to adjust and adapt themselves to various foreign patterns and cultures has minimized their social estrangement. However, the Jews have reaped another alienation, that is to say, if they are not alienated from society, they are cut off from their ancestors and traditional values. The American Jew, it has been observed, is "a marginal man."[3] His adaptation to American life has been through a unique process of 'acculturation' which so far has not meant total assimilation. His is a marginal existence and his struggle is for recognition.

In a world engaged in learning the limitations of intelligence and just coming to grip with man's inability to control the forces of destiny, the Jew, a perpetual victim of history, might be able to speak directly, "in situations of humiliation, nakedness and weakness . . . to the common conviction about the nature of present experience."[4] For Malamud, the Jew has become a special sort of a cultural symbol. He has given his Jews a common identity with mankind. Leslie Field says: "In fact his [Malamud's] Jew may become indistinguishable from the non-Jew as he becomes homogenized in a larger, non-Jewish world. He may emerge as Everyman as his identification with his own peoples' overriding concerns becomes peripheral or marginal."[5] In Malamud's novels, the Jew has certainly become an appropriate symbol of western man searching for his lost roots.

Malamud portrays his protagonists engaged in a struggle with the forces of their cultural and physical environment. He intends to bring forth their hidden strength. Malamud says: "I am more interested in the resources of the spirit, the strength people don't know they have until they are confronted with a crisis."[6]

Bernard Malamud's first novel *The Natural* is a tale of a potential great baseball player, Roy Hobbs, in the big-league world. Here, baseball is a metaphor for the development of consciousness in Roy Hobbs as the 'Jewishness' in Malamud's fiction is a metaphor to connote the twin value of suffering and morality. Malamud uses the professional baseball world to represent larger human issues and does so by giving a mythical treatment to the subject. "Clearly, the game of baseball becomes a metaphor for life. It represents the moral world Roy enters when he joins the Knights."[7] *The Natural*, like all of Malamud's latter novels, is a parable of "the painful process from immaturity to maturity—maturity of attitudes, not of years."[8] What one notices "is this problem, first of representing all that a man intends and plans, and then of getting him not merely to recognize the then of getting him not merely to recognize the countervailing strength of life but to humble himself before it, that is the real situation"[9] in the novel.

Most of Malamud's heroes, when we first meet them, are en route to a new place in search of better prospects—a new life, authenticity and acceptance. In "Pre-game" when we first meet Roy, he is making a train journey for a tryout as a baseball pitcher. His journey takes him through the night "moving toward dawn."[10] Roy is full of high hopes and confident of his talents. Like Narcissus he peers in self-love at his own reflection, "the bright sight of himself" (9) in the berth window. "I feel that I have got it in me—that I am due for something very big" (31) he insists egoistically.

Roy lacks moral integrity. He is egoistic and full of selfish hunger for status, money and good food. Roy, like all of Malamud's heroes, is a puny being in comparison with the mythical archetype he represents. This is because he is a victim of his own selfish needs and desires. Hobbs' name suggests his "hobbled" condition. He is tied down by his own imperfect self which makes him shortsighted towards others. Roy's moral development lies to some extent on his attitude towards his own past experiences and his ability to learn from them. Like Oskar Gassner, the protagonist of Malamud's story "The German Refugee" and Levin of "The Lady of the Lake," Roy tries to escape his dark past and like them eventually realizes the impossibility of doing so. None can escape the limitations of the past, they must acknowledge and overcome them in the present.

Roy's obsession to forget the past is responsible for his not being able to deal with present experience. Having learnt nothing from past suffering, he is doomed to suffer again. Only by accepting the past, he can transcend it. Roy is, however, not courageous enough to accept or even admit his ignominious past. "He recalled a sickening procession of job. . . . He dared not think further" (185). Roy feels "ashamed to be recognized, to have his past revealed like an egg spattered on the floor" (52), so he fiercely guards his past from the prying sports writer, Max Mercy. Roy does not learn from past mistakes. Even in hospital he "hungered in nightmare for quantities of exotic food . . . so they served him a prime hunk of beef and he found it enormously delicious only to discover it was himself he was chewing" (181).

Earlier, too, during the course of his career as a rising star, Roy has in moments of despair yearning for his childhood innocence which he is aware he no longer has. At such moments comes before him the memory of boyhood when he had with "a dog, a stick, an awareness he loved" (111), roamed through green forests. Thus, one senses, along with his quest for fame and wealth, Roy is in search of, "above all, for some lost unity with the self."[11] There are moments when he yearns for "a friend, a father, a home to return to—saw himself packing . . . and running for a train. Beyond the first station he'd be flying Wonderboy out of the window" (131). The crippled child whom Roy (with Iris's help) saves by his one unselfish act is "the image of his own maimed moral innocence."[12] Yet when Memo "destroyed that innocence, symbolized in the episode of running down a child in Roy's new Mercedes,"[13] Roy groans but remains wilfully blind to Memo's destructive nature and Iris's redemptive nature. In the end, however, Roy does overcome his baser self. It is Iris who helps him, "battle past the limitations of bumpton [Hobbs] within."[14] She helps him break out of Memo's evil spell and overcome his own selfishness. She stands once again in the stands, trying to make Roy conscious of his moral responsibility towards his team and his fans.

In this novel, we are initiated to the theme of conflicting nature of man and the need to wilfully assert one's better self over the weaker self. The degree of success that the hero achieves depends upon the choice he makes and to the extent he involves himself with others.

The protagonist in Malamud's *The Assistant* is Frank Alpine who has "lately come from the West, looking for a better opportunity."[15] Frank is haunted by the memories of a loveless childhood and a wasted youth which enjoins him to search for authenticity and acceptance. He wishes to free himself from the determinism of the past, "to clean it out of his self and bring in a little peace, a little order, to change the beginning . . . to change his life before the smell of it suffocated him" (82). Frank Alpine awakens to the possibility of a fuller existence than the one he has been living and that awakening starts his quest for lost roots. Indeed, his struggle is to establish unity with some unacknowledged centre of his personality. Unlike Roy, Frank's ambition is not self-centred and egoistic; he wants to be a better human being and seeks to transcend his old self. The process of reformation is a painful process full of trials.

Malamud depicts Frank's experience of robbing the Jewish grocer not as a presentational event that starts "the drama of personality fulfilling itself."[16] It is Frank's progress and change from the day when he assumes complete control of the store that comprises the dramatic struggle central to the novel. Frank Alpine has both saintly and criminal impulses indicated by his admiration of St. Francis and his association with the criminal Ward Minogue respectively. But Frank is torn by the desire to be saintly like Morris on the one hand and the compulsion to assert his identity by violence like Ward Minogue on the other. His struggle for recognition is thus defined as primarily a struggle between the altruistic and the demonic sides of his character. For Malamud, the gnawing agony in which the ego and the alter ego collide is the most fertile of all subjects. The short history of Frank's life in the store is continually dominated by the yearning of a fractured personality to resolve and so fulfil itself. The measure of Frank's fulfilment and his potential for victory is equated with his submission to others, to a will-breaking responsibility.

For Malamud, man lives in the world of interpersonal relationships, in which he is capable of defining and achieving a satisfactory existence. In the small Jewish segment, Frank seeks satisfactory pattern of relationship with others particularly with the grocer and his daughter Helen. He has totally committed himself to the store and thereby, he accepts poverty and the "alien customs in which a man must live" (60). Frank accepts the burden of Morris Bober, so he emerges as a man capable of human relationship. Frank's acceptance of Judaism is not theological, but signifies his acceptance of responsibility to others—a commitment to human solidarity. Frank's transformation transcends theology, "as the fate of the whole mankind which can only be mitigated when all men assume responsibility for others."[17] In the course of the novel Frank Alpine has moved from a vague anti-Semitism to an acceptance of responsibility for others.

Whereas Morris and his wife Ida regret lost opportunities, Helen wishes to break out of the isolation and forge a meaningful relationship with a person capable of appreciating her worth. Like Frank, she is troubled by the tension between the desire to retain her separate self on the one hand and to end her isolation on the other. Her mechanical existence at home and at work gives her no satisfactory sense of being and the youngmen she meets such as Nat Pearl and Louis Karp value her more as a piece of live furniture to their lives than as an individual. She rejects the materialistic Nat Pearl and in doing so, rejects the prospect of wealth and easy life. But she has the satisfaction of being valued by Frank for her individuality. For Helen, Frank is a "man of possibilities" (93), who holds out for her the possibility of escaping her drab existence and the attentions of the soulless Nat Pearl and the mindless Louis Karp. She realizes that Frank's assault on her in the park was not entirely his fault, but was the result, at least partly, of her apprehension of him. The death of Ward helps her adopt a more sympathetic attitude to him and appreciate his efforts to save her and her mother. This prepares the ground for her subsequent discovery of change in him. She has a glimpse of his sleepless face in the all-night restaurant where he works for the Bobers. She realizes that despite the continuing sameness of his appearance, "he has changed . . . he's not the same man" (215). After this realization of the change in him she accepts his offer and adopts a more relaxed attitude to him.

Morris's chief problem is his own obdurate saintliness. Whenever he chooses to escape from himself, whenever he succumbs to his own opposing self, he immediately suffers reversal. Morris's capacity for sympathetic understanding of another's troubled condition extends to everyone he finds to be the counterpart—from the 'Drunk Woman' who still gets a measure of credit in the store, to All Marcus, the paper products salesman, who was dying of cancer but who refused to give up his routine life. Morris seeks through relationship with others his identity as a sympathetic, honest Jew. He believes that a Jew must be honest at heart. Though he emigrated to America before his conscription to the Tsarist's army but he has got little in that new place. Indeed, this is Malamud's way of indicating that the Jew has still retained his old identity. Morris has endured the pangs and tribulations of life that enabled him to relinquish his self.

Frank, for most part, remains ambivalent, but he achieves at the end unity with the unacknowledged centre of his personality after he recognizes the humanitarian attitude of Morris. The identity Frank ultimately attains is not a new one but one which is refashioned out of the old one by the gradual attenuation of the ego, the cultivation of the altruistic elements in his personality and the acceptance of responsibility for others.

In Malamud's novel *A New Life*, the protagonist S. Levin, like Frank Alpine, is haunted by his desolate and a purposeless wasted youth and a burdensome past. He is a person who has escaped from the easy and arbitrary patterns of ordinary living into a condition of intellectual awareness, of 'active beingness.' What has brought Levin to the West is, in fact, the same determining past that has brought Frank Alpine to rest in the grocery of Bobers. Levin's disaffection with his past and estrangement from society are prominent features of his personality. His struggle is to integrate and find unity with the unacknowledged and unembodied self.

S. Levin is presented as having experienced the characteristic Malamudian protagonist's awakening to the possibility of a new existence. As an Eastern alien, an unacknowledged and underground man, Levin yearns to come above ground to find connection with whatever the world may promise of a new existence. In his conversation with Pauline Gilley, his new chairman's wife, Levin is impelled to reveal something of his innermost self by recounting to her the awakening from a life 'without much purpose.' He says:

> I lived in self-hatred, willing to part with life. . . . But one morning in somebody's filthy cellar, I awoke under burlap bags and saw my rotting shoes on a broken chair. They were lit in dim sunlight from a shaft or window. I stared at the chair it looked like a painting, a thing with value of its own. I squeezed what was left of my brain to understand why this should move me deeply, why I was crying. Then I thought, Levin if you were dead, there would be no light on your shoes in this cellar. I came to believe that I have often wanted to, that life is holy.[18]

This awakening to the possibility of a 'new life' in each of Malamud's protagonists is presented as the beginning of the struggle for recognition and authenticity.

Levin's life as a 'man of principle' was a long stretch of despair until he had another insight when he mentions: "that I was a freeman lit in my mind even as I denied it. I suddenly know as though I was discovering it for the first time that the source of freedom is the human spirit" (178). His trip to the West was in a sense intended to enable him to translate this insight from abstraction into action. But this cannot be accomplished in isolation; he must enter into meaningful relationships with others.

Through his relationship with Pauline Gilley, Levin acquires a knowledge of his true self. Levin and Pauline are both ambivalent in their attitude to each other, as their relation threatens the 'new life' sought by Levin and the security enjoyed by Pauline as the wife of Gerald. Pauline herself is troubled by her infidelity to her husband who despite his lack of idealism and his worship of the 'good life' is kind and generous. Levin is also troubled by his awareness of the gap between the values he preaches and those he practises. As he comes to know from Avis that Pauline and Duffy had been lovers, Levin feels bitter towards her. He thinks that several others had known to this affair while it has been concealed from im. It defeats his ego and he feels an obliteration of his individual self that "he has lost the will to be Levin, that he was, so to say, the extension of Duffy's ghost" (280). He feels a sense of defeat. But he realizes that his identity as a self can be attained only by the attenuation of his ego and Pauline's relation with Duffy does not affect his struggle for recognition.

Though Levin hardly recognizes it, his quest for authenticity and acceptance is obstructed by the ideological environment of Cascadia College. He is manipulated by Gilley and Fabrikant in the context of the departmental election. He becomes a pawn in the game, and his individuality is ignored. It is by the abrasive encounter with Gilley and the rest of the community that the fibre of Levin's self is toughened and the self itself is given a concrete shape. It is ironic that only Gerald, the champion of anti-intellectualism on the campus, is really kind and hospitable to him.

Levin finds in Easchester a blind veneration for statistics and worldly success, compounded by hypocrisy and timidity. Faced with such aridity all around, it is left to Levin to evolve his own set of values from his experience. He is actuated by the urge to deny his past, reflected in his raking the dead leaves in Mrs. Beaty's yard with a maniacal passion as also by the urge to find a new identity as a moral being defined by values and ideals. He feels that "the past hides, but is present" (57). But he realizes that he "must incorporate his devil,"[19] if he is to succeed in his struggle for authenticity and acceptance.

Levin's perpetual estrangement from the values of his environment is heightened by his sense of outrage at discovering 'Bullock's blacklist' containing the names of the instructors supposed to be unsympathetic to the college athletes. While Gilley and Bullock are laced to the "crucial American ritual that binds them to one another and to the culture"[20] by psychic and federal ties, Levin remains apart. His failure to persuade Gilley to rebuke Bullock and make him withdraw the blacklist, results in their drifting apart. As Levin further realizes, the list suggests "a way of life" (280) to which others have become accustomed, but he is not reconciled to it. For him, the temptation to give up the struggle is great and the reward for success is little. Levin does not succeed in the fullest sense of the term, but he does not accept defeat.

In this search for a leader who can be a source of values, Levin turns to Fabrikant expecting him to fight against the list. But Fabrikant regards it, like Gilley, as a question of bread and butter, but not of "our immortal souls" (137). He wishes to use the incident of embarrassing Gilley in the ensuing college election without risking his promotion. Levin's sense of values is not well-defined and his self is not yet sufficiently toughened to make him carry his quarrel with the surrounding culture to the logical conclusion. He is at odds with the 'fun morality' underlying Gilley's and Bullock's attitude to athletes. But Levin lacks the moral energy and the clarity of vision to assert his values against those of the dominant culture.

In contesting for the chairmanship of the English department, Levin accepts responsibility and commits himself to principles. Having made the gesture, he endeavours earnestly to challenge the existing conditions in Cascadia college and work like a zealot for the changes. The intrigues preceding the election temporarily obscured Levin's search for acceptance and authenticity. Gilley's accusation that Levin shows undue haste in trying to reform without understanding sounds plausible, but the danger which Levin perceives, at least, subconsciously is that if he does not act in time, he is likely to accept the values of Easchester and become another Gilley, or more likely, another Fabrikant. His decision to contest for the Chairmanship without any assured support, is no more than an existential gesture against the antihumanistic environment.

Levin's revolt against the forces of anti-liberalism is bound to fail, especially considering his own ambivalent stance towards them. But Levin emerges capable of bearing the responsibilities. His values consist in affirming his personality against the antihumanistic environment of the college. He emerges with a coherent sense of self defined by his commitment to a set of values. Levin achieves identity and recognition by emerging out of "the centripetal isolation of human self"[21] the withdrawal into which had been "the customary American response to the dilemmas of experience."[22] Levin achieves identity by his willing assumption of responsibility for others. Though he is an alienated man, yet in the new place, he forges a connection with his lost roots.

In *The Fixer*, we see the protagonist Yakov Bok, like S. Levin, leaving the *Shtetl*, "to get acquainted with a bit of the world."[23] Yakov reveals to his father-in-law, Samuel, his dissatisfaction with his life in the *Shtetl* and his desire to seek a new life. He says: "I've been cheated from the start. . . . The *Shtetl* is a prison, no change from the day of Khmelmitsky. . . . Here we're prisoners . . . so it's time to try elsewhere I've finally decided" (14). Yakov's decision for change is gradually revealed to his consciousness as the beginning of a struggle for recognition and acceptance.

The fixer's quest for identity manifests itself in his discontent with the precariousness of his existence as a Jew in the *Shtetl* and in going to Kiev in search of a job and experience. At the beginning of his quest, Yakov wishes to be a private self avoiding involvement with others. He starts his quest by first rejecting his Jewish identity and leaving the *Shtetl*. He is a man full of wants he cannot satisfy, "at least, not here" (15). Like Frank Alpine, S. Levin, Yakov Bok is alienated from his past and his self.

His father-in-law, Samuel, pinpoints his lack of charity and discontent with the present. Yakov and Samuel represent the new and the old values in the former's mind. The old man represents the passive acquiescence in the miserable existence of the Jews in Russia. But what Yakov discovers is a meaningless existence that becomes his quest for a 'new life.' Samuel has no thought of leaving the *Shtetl*, nor can he understand the fixer's urge to leave and enter in a hostile world. He embodies the old unquestionable faith in the justice of the Jewish God, while the fixer intends to affirm his individuality and rejects Judaism as well as the Jewish God.

The fervour of Yakov's rejection of Judaism is abated by the first touch of anti-Semitism. When the boatsman ferrying him across the Dnieper indulges in a vicious anti-Semitic tirade, Yakov makes no rejoinder and conceals his Jewishness. Yet, Jewishness haunts him in Kiev where he is more anxious than ever to conceal his religious denomination. While Levin's Westward journey had brought him to the beauty of Cascadia, Yakov's ritual journey lands him in the ugliness and suffocation of Kiev. The anti-Semitism prevalent in Kiev brings to the surface Yakov's urge to deny his Judaism. He assumes a non-Jewish name—Yakov Ivanovitch Dologushev. His efforts to deny his past and his self proves to be futile, and the opportunity sought by him turns out to be one for trapping himself in a more real prison than the *Shtetl*.

Yakov's attitude to experience is ambivalent; he is afraid of the commitment it might involve. This is manifest in the mixture of generosity and caution in his response to the dangerous situation in which he finds the drunken anti-Semitic Nikolai Lebedev. It is only after much trepidation that he saves Lebedev from being suffocated in the snow. At the outset Yakov, like Levin, is confronted with the problem of violating the rules of his new environment. His rescue of the wealthy Lebedev brings him the reward of remunerative employment as an overseer in the brick-works on the outskirts of Kiev. But his acceptance of the position necessitates his living in a quarter prohibited to Jews and, hence, the suppression of his Jewish identity.

Initially Yakov is doubly alienated from the anti-Semitic Russian culture by the fact that he is a Jew, and from Judaism. The denial of his Jewishness is partly necessitated by sheer material necessity in the anti-Semitic society. It is also possible that his rejection of Judaism and his past is in some measure 'an activistic reaction' to the fatalistic acquiescence of old Jewish Samuel.

The quick progress he makes in fixing a job in Kiev appears to be almost a vindication of Yakov's activistic creed. Yakov's denial of his Jewishness and his past are partly reflected in his concealment of his religious denomination and in changing his name. But his new identity hangs on him "like a suit of stolen clothes" (72). His relative affluence makes him feel that he has broken with his past. But the visit of wounded Hasid whom he rescued from violent urchins indicates that Judaism has not relinquished Yakov. His rescue of Hasid is only a humanitarian gesture but it indicates that he retains the essence of Jewishness. But this humanitarian gesture of Yakov is twisted by the authorities later on to foist the charge of 'ritual' murder on him.

Yakov is, at first, 'an invisible man' without an individual identity. It is evident from the fact that all the Jews in Kiev who have relinquished Judaism, it is only Yakov who is charged with 'ritual' murder of the boy Zhenia Golov whose mutilated body is discovered near the brickworks. Residing in the heart of the city he provides a convenient target for the accentuated anti-Semitic feeling of the ignorant and fanatical Russians.

From the moment of his imprisonment, Yakov ceases to exist from the outside world. The decline in the fixer's alienation from the outside world is paralleled by a decline in his alienation from his self. He realizes that at the root of his present miseries lies his pervasive discontent with himself and his existence in the *Shtetl*. He has sought the wrong kind of opportunity, denied himself and brought on himself the intolerable isolation of the solitary cell which makes his life in the Pale appear miserable and comparatively free.

His alienation from the self is reduced further when he realizes the necessity of survival in the face of the attempts by the authorities to kill him by poisoning his food. Their attempts to destroy him reinforce his determination to live and prevail. He discovers a new value in his self and is able to resist the invitations to self-destruction implied in the increasingly harsh conditions of his imprisonment. Yakov's condition as an individual subjected to great psychic strains is paradigmatic of the contemporary human condition. Yakov is convinced of the weakness and cowardice of his persecutors and has developed contempt towards them. Their vacillation makes him determined to live and endure despite his miserable plight.

Yakov's attitude to self and society undergoes a qualitative change through his self-confrontation and introspection during his prolonged imprisonment. He perceives the inhumanity of men like Gurbeshov and Colonel Bodyansky who are controlled by demoniac lust for power. On the other hand, he perceives the basic humanity and essential decency of some of his former fellow-prisoners who had attacked and betrayed him out of incomplete understanding or a misconceived fear of him. This perception is an indication of success for achieving authenticity and acceptance.

Yakov arrives, at the end, at a balance between his urge for personal identity and his human responsibility for the members of the society which he inhabits. The contrary pulls of the self towards isolation and of society towards involvement have attained a delicate equilibrium in the fixer's personality. It is this equilibrium that ultimately defines his identity and enables him to unite with the roots and unacknowledged centre of his personality. Although still imprisoned, we see that Yakov has become a person capable of a fuller and richer life experience.

In *The Tenants*, Malamud does not evade the nightmarish reality of modern experience but, by confronting its irrationality, hopes to use that experience for the purpose of emphasizing the need to overcome the despairing reality and to establish authenticity. Harry Lesser, the protagonist of *The Tenants* lives entombed in the tenement. He lives a half-life somehow knowing the truth but unable to live by it.

Lesser has cut himself off from life and has become the last tenant in a building which is slated to be demolished as soon as his lease runs out. He is callously indifferent to his landlord Levenspiel's pleas to vacate the tenement because it would cause distractions in the conception of the novel he is writing.

Lesser's problem is that he is seeking humanity and identity through writing. He wants "to create love in language and see where it takes him, yes or no. . . . Although if you have to make a journey to trace love down may be you're lost to begin with. No journey will help."[24] Lesser knows the importance of love and still does not heed his heart. Ironically this is also the subject of this incomplete novel, that is to unite with the unacknowledged centre of his personality.

Harry Lesser suffers from a creative block and concerning Lesser's tribulations Malamud has observed: "I like drama of non-productivity, especially where there may be talent. It's an interesting ambiguity, the force of the creative versus the paralysis of life."[25] Thus the conception of Art itself remains moral and it teaches life. It is, however, the insufficient artist who presents, as Malamud puts it the 'soft impeachment' of Art. Lesser's inability to love in life results in his inability to write about love, for Malamud implies that experience is essential for the creative act. Because Lesser leads an incomplete life, he is unable to complete his work. Reflecting on his friend Lazar Kohn's work, Lesser concludes it is an incomplete work of an incomplete man and he feels an affinity with Kohn. He imagines Kohn's thought: "I can't give you more than I have given you—make you more than you are—because I haven't presently got it to give and don't want anyone to know, least of all myself" (88).

Willie learns something about the craft of writing under Lesser's tutelage but he also learns to suffer Lesser's agonies at writing. As Lesser had done, Willie renounces life and lives in isolation to devote his time to his book. Lesser's life undergoes a change too. He adopts, at least temporarily, Willie's more instinctual self which he has kept suppressed. The exchange of certain characteristics is, in fact, Lesser's "confrontation of the insulated self with the acher, its repressed 'other.'"[26]

Lesser as master in the craft of writing criticizes Willie's lack of aesthetic of form in his writing, and he also criticizes Willie's use of his ethnicity as the basis of his art, when he points out that black should be "more than colour or culture" (54) and further tells Willie: "you can't turn black experience into literature just by writing it down" (60). Willie finds such criticism contrived to be Semitic prejudice against the blacks. Moreover, "Willie has turned the politic of a group into an object himself, black man. In Willie Art is Politics. Politics is Art."[27] Willie is not just a man but a black man and his self-declared form serves hatred and vengeance. His form prescribes that black culture can arise only through destruction of Jewish culture. Initially, before Lesser hurts his pride, writing 'black' for Willie meant relating a poignant tale of his unhappy childhood in the ghetto. Now writing 'black' is for vengeance against Jews. He has happy thoughts of pogroms. Art and politics are one for him now and he expects his book to serve his political purpose. Malamud desires, however, that art have moral concerns. It must promote love and brotherhood and as a result he cannot complete his book; he can only 'create festering lives.'

Willie and Lesser stand for a conflict between two different races and two different concepts of art. The novel nears its end with the black and the Jew hacking away at each other. In desperation they lock in a deadly embrace and yet ironically it is an act of mutual "interanimate each other in a community of pain."[28] Hence, symbolically both of them encounter their lost roots and exhibit their struggle for recognition.

After *The Tenants*, Malamud comes to William Dubin and writes about the problems of middle-aged biographer to uphold his commitment to life. In *Dubin's Lives*, the protagonist, William B. Dubin is an inward, self-fastened man. He believes that he has inherited "an inclination to a confined, lonely life,"[29] from his father. His mother had gone mad after the death of her younger son by drowning and she had died when Dubin was only thirteen. His feeling of loneliness stems from his childhood which had been lacking in emotional warmth and security. The basic issue in the novel is a "life battling with it self and effects of time—the effects of aging, the loneliness and paralysis of a long marriage, the desire for a new life."[30]

After his mother's death, Dubin's only company at home was his father, so he "missed a feminine presence in the house. I missed a woman. I tried to appease this lack by often falling in love" (45). Dubin's marriage, however, is not inspired by love, it is an arrangement. He marries Kitty, a non-Jewish widow, and the marriage is fairly satisfied but only as an arrangement, not as a merger of souls. Now, in his middle age, Dubin wonders whether marriages do not go on for too long, and whether they should not best be ended by mutual consent, which might be refreshing for both partners. "He wanted another chance in marriage; he could do it better than he had done it. And he'd his bride's first husband" (182). His wife keenly feels his apartness from her. Unable to reach him, she says helplessly, "you're out on your private little back sailboat in the rough green sea and here I am alone on a dreary lava-like shore" (162). Dubin gives

Kitty little both emotionally and physically. Dubin is aware of his lack of love:

> It isn't easy to give if you're anchored in an involved subjectivity. Some people complicate their feelings in self-protective ways. I must be one of them. You think you're sailing with a cargo of love, but never deliver because you haven't hoisted anchor, although you have the illusion you had. (372)

Dubin's sense of isolation is deepened by oncoming old age, his impotence with his wife and the fact that his children have fledged: "Overnight, it had seemed, they had changed and gone, each to pursue an unpredictable destiny. Who would have thought so, contemplating them as kids? Yes, you said love, they said love, but each lived a world apart" (188).

He talks of the need to live life "to the hilt" and asserts: "one recovers of youth only what he can borrow from the young" (64). Thus Dubin plunges into an affair with youthful Fanny Bick as his right to experience a rejuvenating experience "before he was too old to enjoy it" (316). He looks upon Fanny as a "break water against age, loss of vital energy, the approach of death" (287). Alive, promiscuous Fanny restores Dubin's self-confidence and his hopes for a new life. She helps him get rid of his self-recriminations. As Fanny gives Dubin release from stagnation, he with his knowledge of many lives helps her grow from adolescent sexuality into mature womanhood. Fanny looks upon Dubin as lover, father, friend and he helps her to become a lot more serious about herself. No longer wanting to let life drift along, she seeks stability in her relationship and herself feels more confident about her ability to reorganize her life. She gives totally to Dubin and expects more commitment from him.

Dubin's rejuvenating affair does not help to open him up; on the contrary, it distances him further from his family. In loving Fanny he withholds love from his wife and daughter. Moreover, by Malamudian rules, no gain is without loss. Dubin gains favour with Fanny, but loses stability in his life. He wants to cheat the aging aspect of time by taking up with Fanny. Because of her youthfulness, Fanny represents a bright future. It is Kitty, with her constant thoughts of the lived life, who represents the past. Dubin's major problem is to reconcile his commitments towards Kitty (his past) and yet enjoy the potential of the future that Fanny offers, in his attempt to start a new life at such a late age. His quest for a new life, however, merely reinforces the hold of the past. Dubin has to learn to accept the dilapidation that time wroughts, for "what life is trying to teach him is the truth about time; its erosions, its duplicities, what is recoverable from it, and what isn't and above all how one can outwit it and how one can't."[31]

Dubin's efforts at self-discovery and recognition are closely related to his quest to write a biography of D.H. Lawrence. Through his biographies Dubin feels he learns how to live life, "Biography . . . teaches you the conduct of life. Those who write about life reflect about life . . . you see in other who you are" (149). He himself leads a confined, lonely life so as to write lives. Malamud has justified Dubin's want for isolation when at work: "Isolation is an important drama for any writer . . . you have to shut yourself out of the variety of life."[32] Dubin, however, takes his isolation to extremes. It only helps build up his already inflated self-esteem and cuts him off from lived life. He has no friends, colleagues or for that matter, binding relationships with his colossal narcissism. Dubin, in total selfishness, makes emotional demands on others but isolates himself when it suits him. Like Fidelman and Lesser, Dubin, in pursuit of his profession, leads a narrow, regulated life. He makes a prison of his own through his repetitive demands to any sort of communication with the world outside. There are moments when he feels, "I'm like a rock with an iron fence around it" (330). Dubin could admit that his prison, as that of S. Levin, is really his own flawed self from which there seems no escape to freedom. Dubin needs to reconcile the conflicting demands of his work and life as also within himself.

In his last novel, *God's Grace*, Malamud tackles the big questions of existence and authenticity that have informed his earlier works. The novel is dire warning against the force within us that drives us, literally, to destroy ourselves. The novel opens the day after nuclear war has destroyed civilization and all mankind. However, the protagonist Cohn survives to struggle against that invisible force of evil in the soul that has led man to destroy himself. He discovers another example of God's absentmindedness—a young chimpanzee who is well-versed in human speech and abstract thought. Cohn thinks: "Survive is what we have to do. Thus we protest our fate to God and at the same time imitate Him."[33] After the initial shock and anger at the total devastation of all life subsides, Cohn rationalizes:

> God made man seriously imperfect. Maybe what was on His mind was that if He made man whole, pacific good, he would feel no need to become better, and if he didn't, he would never truly be a man. He also planned it that man had to contend with evil, or it was no go. But the awful thing was that the evil was much bigger bag of snakes than man could handle. We behaved toward each other like animals, and therefore the Second Flood followed hard on the Day of Devastation. (73)

Thus Cohn analyzes man's ambivalent nature, more prone to evil than good, and the cause of his fall from God's grace. Understanding of the deficient human nature makes Cohn conscious of the need for self-betterment. He ponders: "Man had innumerable chances but was—in the long run—insufficient to God's purpose. He was insufficient to himself . . . he never mastered his animal nature for the good of all . . . nor could he invent a workable altruism. In short, he behaved too often irrationally, unseasonably, savagely, beastially" (124).

Gradually a few chimpanzees, a lonely gorilla and finally a family of baboons and a shadowy albino ape appear on the island, somehow having survived the nuclear fire and the flood that followed. Cohn wonders if god has granted a new lease to life to flourish by allowing the handful of animals to live on, or did they also attest to God's 'cosmic absentmindedness.' With pleasure Cohn discovers that the family of chimpanzees easily acquire human language and are receptive to human thought, "a stupendous miracle" (100). Cohn organizes a *seder* to celebrate the emergence of speech among the apes and to express sincere gratitude to God for sustaining them through adverse circumstances and for the bountiful life on the island. However, in *God's Grace*, the primates not only talk, each has a telling name and distinctive traits. Thus Malamud gives them an individuality which does credit to the author's creative ability. "Indeed the theme of language as sanctified is so central to *God's Grace* that speech seems to exist not just as the product of cerebration and the proper physical organs but as a moral power in the very structure of reality."[34] Now that a common language exists between the chimps and himself Cohn hopes to establish a functioning community. He starts a school to educate the perspective chimpanzees. They show polite interest as he orates, though how much they absorb even Cohn is not too sure. However, as his teachings register, the chimpanzees become orderly and gainfully employed. They learn to live by the rules and regulations of the island for the mutual benefit of all.

Though the island community shows much promise but things go haywire as past prejudices surface once again in the new world. Intolerance towards others, the bane of the lost civilization, sets in. Buz cannot bring himself to even tolerate the lonesome gorilla, George. "He's fot (sic) stupid pig, and besides that he stinks" (78), states Buz. Likewise, all the chimps are hostile towards the baboons—they "don't belong to our tribe" (168). Like Buz, though all the apes adopt human speech, imitate Cohn's ways and obey the rules laid down by him, they, nonetheless, assert their individuality and also their 'otherness' in comparison to the homo sapian Cohn. Thus greed, selfishness and jealousy undermines the possibilities Cohn had imagined. His optimism about a new, responsible society, proves to be delusive. As the restraints that Cohn had imposed upon them by way of admonitions and his authority as the leader crumble, the apes assert their freedom by indulging in cannibalism and infanticide. The apes kill and devour the baboon children Sara and Pat and finally even Cohn's little daughter Rebekah is killed.

In the denouement, the primates indulge in an orgy of inhuman brutality. As evil prevails, God withdraws His grace and the chimps lose their power of speech. The end reminds us very closely of the gruesome ending to *The Tenants* where Willie

Spearmint slashes off Lesser's testicles with a sharp knife and at that moment Lesser drives an axe into Willie's head. Cohn, in *God's Grace*, is also incarcerated by the chimps and finally immolated. "Here again Malamud is back on familiar turf, dramatizing physical and spiritual torment, a fertile vein in his imagination and a valve of his philosophy."[35] In Malamud's world good intentions are not good enough. Cohn is expected to practise selflessness which he fails to do when he takes up with Mary Madelyn, hence the unhappy conclusion becomes inevitable, and he is not able to dig roots.

Each of Malamud's work is concerned with the 'being' of the central character with his decision to discover a new life, acceptance and authenticity, with the subject-matter of the search which in every case begins with the search for self and the lost roots. Malamud has elaborated in his short stories the protagonist's struggle for recognition and acceptance. It is their inauthentic existence which goads them to search for an authentic life.

## II

In *The Magic Barrel*, Malamud tries to exhibit "an affirmation of man's ability to realize himself, even in the face of deprivation and disaster."[36] The story, "The First Seven Years," reveals Malamud's apprentice character engaged "in the process of changing his fate [and] his life."[37] The 'dreams of a better life' seem to provide the central theme in the story, adumbrated right at the outset: "Feld, the shoemaker, was annoyed that his helper, Sobel, was so insensitive to his reverie that he wouldn't for a minute cease his frantic pounding at the other bench."[38] Feld, the Polish Jew in New York, remembers his wasted youth, wishes he had a boy instead of a daughter, and almost adores Max, the peddler's son, who tries to further his education. Miriam, his daughter, though reads the classics that Sobel suggests her to read. Feld tells Max about his daughter's qualities when the former comes to his shop. Somehow, Sobel hears the negotiations between Feld and Max, he rushes out of the shop and does not return to work for the shoemaker. The new assistant Max is dishonest and unreliable. Even Miriam is not interested in him and she tells Feld about Max, "he's nothing more than a materialist. . . He's only interested in things" (16). Feld picks up the courage to meet Sobel and asks him to come back to work. It is at this moment that Sobel tells him that he had been working for the shoemaker only with a hope to marry Miriam. He explains to Feld that the girl already knew about it. The shoemaker marvels at his assistant's devotion and experiences a transformation in his inner attitude towards Sobel, Miriam and the idea of 'a better life.' It is this dimension of faith in the possibility of ' a new life' that challenges the deterministic hold on life.

In "The Mourners" the problem of poverty and social responsibility recurs more insistently. At sixty-five, Kessler, "formerly an egg candler, lived alone on social security" (21). Thirty years back, he abandoned his wife and children in order to live alone in his own manner, but the guilt of desertion does not let him live in peace. In a decrepit tenement on the East Side, he has a flat on the fifth floor, but even with the immediate neighbours he has little communication. Only Ignance, the janitor, knows him well, and upbraids him for the garbage he throws on the stairs. Ignance reports to Gruber, the landlord, against the insanitary conditions in Kessler's flat. Despite Gurber's warning, Kessler does not move out of the flat till he is bodily dragged down by the Marshall. He is picked up by his neighbour, the Italian woman, and is brought back to his flat. The landlord is totally amazed at Kessler's conduct and wants to tell him that he should not exasperate a person with high blood pressure. But it is Kessler who sounds more convincing, "who hurts a man without a reason? Are you a Hitler or a Jew?" (26) He later tells Gurber about his remorse at having walked out on his family. Thereafter, Kessler sits on the floor and starts mourning because he fears that the tenant was mourning the landlord. The way Feld had the epiphany about Sobel's love, Gurber too sinks to the floor and becomes another mourner. It is obvious that both of them are mourning the loss of human feeling—Kessler for forsaking his family and Gurber for treating the tenant in a harsh manner.

The story "The Girl of My Dreams" deals with the dream of a young creative writer, Mitka, and his disillusionment with a fellow writer. Mitka burns in despair the manuscript of his novel rejected by twenty publishers on which he had spent three long years. He shuts himself in a room and rejects the amorous entreaties of Mrs. Lutz, the landlady, who herself is a creative writer. Once Mrs. Lutz tries to lure Mitka out of the room with the information that on his floor has arrived Beatrice, a new guest who writes, but Mitka is totally indifferent to the talent of this new writer. Malamud seems to suggest in the failure of Mitka that art need not be littered with symbols because a surfeit of classical allusions hinders communicability.

Malamud seems to be conscious of the complex pattern of relationship between Jews and Blacks that he has exhibited in the novel *The Tenants*, "Black Is My Favorite Colour" and "Angel Levine." In the story "Angel Levine" he produces a black Jew. Like Feld, the shoemaker, Manischevitz, is a tailor who "in his fifty-first years suffered many reversals and indignities" (43). His wife Fanny, bed-ridden with the hardening of arteries, is nearing death. One day in the living room he finds sitting Alexander Levine, the black Jew, whom the tailor refuses to believe. After asking pointed questions to authenticate the divinity of the visitor, Manischevitz asks Levine about the wings, and gets this answer: "Under certain circumstances we lose privileges and prerogatives upon returning to earth, no matter for what purpose, or endeavouring to assist whosoever" (46). Levine says that he lives in Harlem, and just at that moment Manischevitz feels stronger and notices tangible improvement even in Fanny's condition. Then trouble returns, his life becomes more unbearable. Then he sets out in search of Levine and finds the black angel sitting in a saloon involved in an amorous encounter with a 'big-breasted Negress.' Being disgusted with the conduct of the black angel, he returns to berate God, and suddenly one afternoon dreams of Levine with wings. He visits Levine again and apologizes to him for his scepticism. He sees the black wings through a small broken window as Levine enters a room. On return he finds Fanny wielding the dust mop, and is overwhelmed by the miracle. If a Jew is a metaphor for humanity, then the implication of Manischevitz's observation is evident; there are human beings in every religion and ethnic group even if they look outwardly different.

In "The Lady of the Lake," the quality of personal integrity is tested because the motivation behind Henry Levin's pilgrimage to Italy is sheer romantic adventurism. In order to reject his Jewish past he starts calling himself Henry B. Freeman, and reaches Stresa to admire the beauty of Lake Maggiore. The padrona of the pension he stays at suggests that he should visit Isola Del Dongo, the island famous for its beauty. There he meets the girl of his dreams rising out of the lake. "Her dark, sharp Italian face had that quality of beauty which holds the mark of history, the beauty of people and civilization" (101). When she asks whether he is a Jew, he denies it, hoping that the denial would impress her. He tries to rationalize his lie by affirming that "a man's past was, it could safely be said, expandable" (113). When he follows her naked in the lake, he little realizes that she would have known the fact of his Jewishness. She deflates him by confessing the truth that her name is Isabella della Seta, and she belongs to the family of the caretakers of the palace. After the initial shock, Henry realizes that both of them had lied to each other, he heroically declares his love irrespective of her social status, she again asks him: "Are you a Jew?" and Henry's answer is: "How many no's make never? Why do you persist with such foolish question?" (118). At that moment she unbuttons her bodice, and Henry notices the act of the Nazis at Buchenwald; to his horror, "he discerned tattooed on the soft and tender flesh a bluish line of distorted number" (119). She explains then her inability to marry him: "We are Jews. My past is meaningful to me. I treasure what I suffered for" (119). Before he comes out with his belated confession, Isabella vanishes among the statues. Malamud brings forth the absurdity of disowning one's past in order to masquerade as a free individual, a problem central to the personality of Henry Levin.

The story "Idiots First" deals with Mendel and his idiot son, Issac. It is an impressive account of the destitution and human responsibility. Mendel is anxious to send his son to uncle Leo in California who would look after the handicapped boy. Mendel wants to arrange the train fare, for that he parts away with his gold watch; he could get only eight dollars from the pawnbroker. With a broken heart he goes to Fishbein, the philanthropist Jew, who refuses to, "contribute to personal pleasure trips. . . . I never give to unorganized charity."[39] In a depressed state Mendel goes to the rabbi who is himself penniless, but asks Mendel to take away his fur-lined coat and sell it, though the circumstances in which he snatches the coat from the screaming wife of the rabbi are painfully comic. At the gate to the station stands Ginzberg, Mendel's old acquaintance, and a veritable spectre of death. He refuses to open it, for though the train is late, it was 'supposed' to have left by the time Mendel and Issac reach the station. When Mendel asks him to explain the meaning of responsibility, Ginzburg utters, "To create conditions. To make what happens. I ain't in the anthropomorphic business" (13). When reminded of the value of pity, he rattles off a snappy answer: "This ain't my commodity. The law is law—the cosmic universal law . . . the one I got to follow myself" (13). Mendel's account of his past and the present predicament fails to move Ginzburg, till Mendel clutches him by the throat and asks: "You bastard, don't you understand what it means human?" (14). Mendel puts Issac on the train, embraces him and advises him to help uncle Leo. When the train leaves, Mendel returns to the stairs to see "what had become of Ginzburg" (15).

The action turns on Mendel's desperate determination to fend off his pursuer until he can get his imbecile son on a train to California kinsman. It shows that humans can defy inevitability; even fate may be humanized and life snatched from death. Sheldon Harshinow asserts: "Unlike 'The Mourners' in which Malamud puts a grotesque character into a realistic setting, in 'Idiots First' he places comparatively real characters into grotesque setting. The effect produces a disquieting blurring of the line between reality and fantasy. We don't know how much of action 'really' happens and how much exists in Mendel's desperately fearful imagination. The epiphany produces a shock that slowly turns to admiration as we realize we have before us a seriocomic parable of human pain and possibility."[40]

What is non-human in the story seems malevolently resistant to Mendel's attempt to assert the human in the inhuman world we inhibit. One of the Critics asserts, "'Idiots First' strikes me as Malamud's most heightened plea for human possibility. Mendel is pitted against natural law, the physical world, and contemporary manners."[41]

The story "Black Is My Favorite Color" presents the racial problem between Blacks and Jews. Nat Lime, the narrator in the story, is a forty-four year old bachelor, who runs a liquor store in Harlem. He talks of his 'fate with colored people' for he has passed through some agonizing situations concerning the prejudices that blacks nurse against Jews, though black remains still his 'favorite color.' Nat has made genuine overtures of friendship towards the coloured but the result has always been disappointing.

Nat wistfully remembers his childhood friend, Buster Wilson whom he would take to the movies and offer his books and candies. He is aware of the violence which can erupt at any moment in Harlem, and remembers one incident in which Buster's drunkard father was involved. Almost of the same age as Huckleberry Finn when he is shocked by the bloody feud between the Grangerfords and the Shepherdsons, Nat is equally horrified at the sight of blood streaming from the battered nose of Buster's father. Once when Nat asks him why he does not wait for him after the shows, Buster remains quiet, and one day without any provocation he hits Nat in the teeth: "Because you are a Jew bastard. Take your Jew movies and your Jew candy and shove them up your Jew ass" (22).

After this traumatic initiation into the terror of racial antagonism, Nat continues his search for friendship with blacks. When he tries to be nice to a black lady, Mrs. Ornita Harris, she tells him that she wants no favour from white men. When Nat wins Ornita's confidence after giving her discount on liquor, he wishes to go ahead with his plans to marry her, but he is assaulted by black boys when he accompanies Ornita to her place.

To his appeals of human brotherhood, their response is of severe accusation against 'a Jew landlord.' After all these painful failures, Nat muses: "That's how it is. I give my heart and they kick me in my teeth" (31). This monologue of Nat Lime is a prolonged lament over the different ways in which blacks have rejected his offer of assistance, friendship and love.

In "The Death of Me," Malamud takes up the problem of communication between two persons of the same religious community. What Malamud seems to convey is that the deadlock in human relationships is not always because of different racial attitudes but also because of opposing individual oddities of temper. Instead of being parochial towards Jews, Malamud handles them as severely as he would treat the non-Jews. Marcus, the clothier, has two assistants and all three are immigrant Jews. Josip Bruzak, the presser, is from Poland, whereas Emilio Vizo, the tailor, is a Sicilian. They are excellent at their respective jobs, and Marcus tries to persuade them to live in peace with each other. Josip remembers his wife and son whereas Emilio has a bully in his wife who often leaves him.

Since Marcus intervenes, they abandon their plans to assault each other with crude weapons. Marcus partitions the room with a view to isolating them, but they are soon at each other's throat, and despite his intervention seriously wound each other. This scene results in a heart attack to the clothier. The story narrates man's indifference to man, precisely for the reason that he fails to work out a viable pattern of human relationship. It is the withering away of compassionate understanding of one another that ruins the possibility of a dialogue in life.

In "The German Refugee," Malamud deals with Oskar Gassner, the German refugee, who flees the Nazis and come to America. The story is related through Martin Goldberg whom Oskar hires to learn English. Oskar is a reputed writer and critic in German, and his assignment in America is to deliver a lecture at the institute of Public Studies. He leaves Germany and his gentile wife when the Nazis start shattering the Jewish stores and Synagogues. Conscious of his difficulty with English language, Oskar is often depressed at the prospects in New York. Martin tries to teach him in a patient manner, and notices the promise in Oskar. At that moment Oskar is indignant at the political turbulence in his country. Despite his sincere efforts to write down his lecture in English or in German, he fails to complete even the first sentence and this results in his psychic breakdown. Elaborating his handicap Oskar remarks: "I have lozt faith. I do not—not longer possezz (sic) my former value of myself. In my life there has been too much illusion" (206). Martin is scared at Oskar's state of mind, and then is signed the Soviet-Nazis-non-aggression pact which further rattles Oskar's mind. Despite this political development and his uneasy account of life with his gentile wife, Oskar delivers an impressive lecture on Whitman. But to Martin's utter disbelief, Oskar commits suicide, and the genesis is traced to a letter from Oskar's mother-in-law. She had mentioned that after Oskar left his wife got converted to Judaism, as a result of which the Brown Shirts shot her in the head and toppled her "into an open tank ditch, with the naked Jewish men, their wives and children, some Polish soldiers, and a handful of gypsies" (212).

In all these stories Malamud seems to be concerned with the problem of comprehension of life. By rejecting the opportunity to understand fellow-beings, men embitter their lives through an idiotic pursuit of narrow self-interest. In their persistence to remain morally impervious, they "cannot connect with one another."[42]

The next collection *Pictures of Fidelman* is an episodic novel consisting of six stories. "In each chapter, Fidelman pursues a different kind of artistic endeavour, lives (after two chapters in Rome) in a different Italian city (Milan, Florence, Naples and Venice) and loses a different part of his American values."[43] Arthur Fidelman discovers that both art and self are quite different from what he thought them to be.

In "Last Mohican," having failed as a painter, Fidelman turns to art history. Fidelman's flaw is his effort to create for himself an identity by repudiating his Jewish past and need for mutual responsibility. Fidelman as yet has no faith in anything beyond the urgencies of the hungers of the self. But in Malamud's world, a real 'new life' involves a radical change of attitude towards the self and others. "The search for a new freedom usually ends in an imprisoning tangle of relationships and commitments and responsibilities. The attempt to deny time and evade the impingements of history yields reluctantly and painfully to the discovery that . . . to be born is to be born into history."[44] However, we also know that "Malamud's uprooted protagonist continually seeks forgetfulness through cultural metamorphosis."[45] What Fidelman has to learn is that he cannot escape Susskind's demand for charity without diminishing his own humanity. Being Jewish makes him, out of historical necessity, responsible for his fellow Jews. Fidelman has rejected his Jewish history in favour of Roman history. However, to deny one's past is to deny oneself a good future. But as other Malamud's characters have done, so will Fidelman, through his irresponsibility, initiate the painful process that will lead him to self-recognition and achieve authenticity.

In "Still Life" Fidelman is back to his previously abandoned attempt to be a painter. He rents a part of a woman artist's studio to pursue his art and the story traces his progress as painter and lover. Being a *Schlemiel*, Fidelman has a penchant for lucklessness and in winning the landlady's heart. Fidelman, "ever a sucker,"[46] strangely lusts for the cold, business-minded pittrice, Annamaria Oliovino, and pays for the privilege of loving her by being a slave to her. Fidelman's love is selfish and lustful, therefore it blocks his artistic energy. Unable to work he suffers much, and in quest for meaningful life, he wanders the streets of Rome. Then, suddenly he was "struck by a thought if you could paint his sight; give it its quality in yours, the spirit belonged to you. History becomes aesthetic!" (43) It is a labour of love, therefore he succeeds in catching the immediate likeness of Annamaria in paint, and because art, love and life are inextricably woven together, Fidelman inadvertently penetrates the secret of Annamaria's soul; she had borne a child incestuously conceived, whom she has murdered (thereby the irony of the title "still life").

In "The Naked Nude," Fidelman finds himself in bondage to two Milan crooks who save him from being arrested by the police for pick-pocketing. The condition for freedom that they offer is that Fidelman reproduce the Titan painting of Venus of Urbino and help them steal the original from a nearby museum. Fidelman hesitates to steal from another painter but his captors assure him that it is the way of life, "Art steals and so does everybody . . . it's the way of world. We're only human." (58). Aware that only compliance will get him his freedom, Fidelman agrees.

It was five years after "Naked Nude" that Malamud took up Fidelman's history again in "A Pimp's Revenge." Once again we find Fidelman trying to work out the relationship between art and life, a recurrent theme in *Pictures of Fidelman*. Each story focuses on the relationship so that Fidelman's failure as artist is inextricably linked with his failure as a person. For Malamud, the postulates of art and life are identical. The imperatives of art, as of life, must not merely deal with aesthetics, but with moral purposes as well. Malamud says: "Art tends towards morality. It values life, even when it doesn't it tends to . . . Art in essence celebrates life and gives us our measure."[47] This is the message of *Pictures of Fidelman* and this is the lesson that Susskind had tried to inculcate in Fidelman so that he can attain acceptance and authenticity. Sheldon Harshinow avers:

> Fidelman's self-discovery is begun but by no means complicated in the first story. As his comic adventures continue, Fidelman has layer after layer of superficial identity stripped away; episode by episode he slowly discovers a new dimension of identity as craftsman and lover. He learns to invent life as he ceases to imitate what he thinks is art. . . . Susskind is really Fidelman's alter-ego, representing a part of himself he would like to ignore. Fidelman is, then, symbolically pitted against himself. In the final episode of the last story, as in the opening one, we see that the acceptance of Fidelman's hidden self requires an expression of mercy, love, charity, or forgiveness to confirm his faith in himself and humanity.[48]

In *Rembrandt's Hat*, Malamud captures the ambivalence of human nature and spiritual isolation that ultimately leads to the failure of communication. In "The Silver Crown," Albert Gans, a high school biology teacher whose father is dying of cancer, visits a faith healer, Rabbi Jonas Lifschitz. The doubtful son agrees to have the healer prepare a crown of melted silver designed and blessed in a way that can miraculously restore health. The Rabbi assures him that the crown must be made "individual for your father. Then his health will be restored. There are two prices."[49] Albert impulsively orders for the more expensive crown, but after paying nine hundred and eighty six dollars, he suffers a change of heart and decides that he has been tricked by a clever man using hypnosis. Rushing back to the rabbi's dingy apartment, Albert demands the return of his money. The Rabbi advises him not to doubt God's powers. When Albert finally bursts out at the Rabbi's chicanery, he also overcomes the sentiments of duty towards his father and declares: "He hates me. . . . I hope he croaks" (30). The Rabbi points a finger at God in heaven and calls Albert a murderer. An hour afterwards dies Albert's father in the hospital.

It is not pointed out in the story whether Jonas Lifschitz believes in his own powers or is simply a conman. But it is he who gives voice to the story's spiritual truths. When Albert asks whether he believes in the crown's power in order for it to work, the Rabbi replies that everyone has doubts: "We doubt God and God doubts us. . . . I am not afraid so long as you love your father" (15). Only love and compassion can help overcome the uncertainty of life. Without them spiritual growth is impossible. In the end it is Albert who reveals himself as the charlatan whose self-deception possibly has prevented a miracle.

The story "The Letter" conveys the pain of life and its locale is a mental hospital. Whenever Newman comes to see his father at the gate, he sees Teddy with a letter in his hand which he wants to be mailed. Newman finds the letter is not written; it is just a blue envelope with white paper inside. Having lost their mental balance, both Teddy and his father are in the hospital. When Newman insists that the letter should contain some contents and an address, Ralph asks him whether he had been in war. When the answer is in the negative, Ralph understands the difference between his world and the world of Newman. What

Malamud seems to convey through Ralph's empty, unwritten letter is the human anxiety to be connected with the world. Robert Solotaraff writes:

> The presence or absence of letters is a recurrent motif in *Rembrandt's Hat* tales of 'baffled communication.' There are the unmailed blank pages in 'The Letter' and 'In Retirement' Dr. Morris's letter to a much younger woman—a letter that earns him considerable derision and pain. In 'Notes from a Lady at a Dinner Party' Max Alder is intrigued, sexually inflamed, and then humiliated by the barrage of little letters that Karla Harris, his dinner party hostess, keeps slipping into his pockets.[50]

In "My Son the Murderer" the focus is on the failure of communication between Leo and his son, Harry. They are strangers to each other, for Harry rarely comes out of his room; he refuses to accept employment and waits for the draft order. Harry is distrustful of the societal intrigues around him. Leo explains his helplessness, "The way he frightens my wife and she is glad to go to my daughter's house early in the morning to take care of the three children. I stay with him in the house but he don't talk to me" (128). This credibility gap is equally wide between Moe Berkman, Leo's friend, and his daughters who add to Moe's 'worries and anxieties.' Leo does not know how to reach his son's mind, how to involve him in a meaningful dialogue with him or the world. He reads his son's letters with a view to arrive at the cause of his sickness, but finds nothing suggestive, except a reminder from a girl to return her books and a note from the draft board. Harry catches his father reading the girl's letter and that confirms his suspicion that his father always spies on him. He threatens to kill his father and leaves the house to drown himself at the Coney Island. Harry says that he is frightened of the world and Leo pleads that Harry should have mercy on the old man. When the story finishes, Harry is still standing with his feet in the ocean and Leo still cajoling him to desist from the desperate measure.

Though there is immense gloom in life, Malamud seems to suggest that one should not reject life but accept its harshness. Nihilism neither minimizes misery nor remedies it. In all the stories of *Rembrandt's Hat*, failure of communication causes lack of understanding or vice-versa. Malamud condemns the life-negating factors like absence of communication and affirms a positive view of life.

In *Rembrandt's Hat*, if there is anything new in this collection of stories, it is the widower who outnumbers the young and the married people. In earlier works such a large number of old men do not appear and it would be worthwhile to suggest that the ultimate point in the quest for a new life in Malamud's protagonists lies in facing the inevitable old age, the spasmodic remembrance of youth, the difficulty of adjustment with posterity and the eternal problem of personal dignity and freedom. The situation in which Malamud involves his bachelors and widowers in *Rembrandt's Hat* tends to affirm his earlier announcement that he is writer in defence of man who seeks recognition, acceptance and authenticity.

Malamud has emphasized that he bases all of his writing on a belief in the nobility of the human spirit. He often succeeds in showing us the human soul, stripped bare of romantic dreams, pretence, and materialistic aspirations in conflict with its own divided nature. Frank Alpine's encounter with Morris Bober, Leo Finkle's quest for a bride turning into a quest for his own identity, Fidelman's experiences with refugee, Schnorrer and Yakov Bok's encounter with the anti-Semitic gentile world—all lead them to self-discovery and to final integration with their authentic self. Therefore, in Malamud's fiction, freedom can be achieved but only through moral awareness which binds a person to other in a web of commitments. The next chapter deals with the problem of exile and alienation, and eventually comes to conclusion showing the ways how the protagonist integrates and commits himself with others.

## NOTES

1. Richard Lehan, "Existentialism in Recent American Fiction: The Demonic Quest," *Recent American Fiction: Some Critical Views*, ed. Joseph J. Waldmeir (Boston: Little, Brown, 1963) 64.

2. Lionel Trilling, *Freud and the Crisis of Our Culture* (Boston: Houghton Muffin, i962) 293.
3. C. Bezalel Sherman, *The Jew within American Society: A Study in Ethnic Individuality* (Chicago: Univ. of Chicago Press, 1961) 32.
4. Benjamin Demot, "Jewish Writers in America" *Commentary*, 31 (1961) 130.
5. Leslie Field, "Bernard Malamud and the Marginal Jew," *The Fiction of Bernard Malamud*, ed. Richard Astro and Jackson J. Benson (Corvallis: Oregon State Univ. Press, 1977) 109.
6. Haskel Frankel, "Interview with Bernard Malamud," *Saturday Review* (Sept. 10, 1996) 23.
7. Sheldon J. Hershinow, *Bernard Malamud* (New York: Atlantic, Frederick Unger, 1980) 23.
8. Tony Tanner, *City of Words: American Fiction 1950-1970* (New York: Harper and Row, 1971) 323.
9. Alfred Kazin, *Contemporaries* (New York: Atlantic, Little, Brown, 1962) 219.
10. Bernard Malamud, *The Natural* (Harmondsworth: Penguin, 1952) 9.
11. Levies K. Grieff, "Quest and Defeat in *The Natural*" *Thoth*, 8 (1967) 23.
12. Robert Ducharme, *Art and Idea in The Novels of Bernard Malamud: Towards "The Fixer"* (The Hague: Mouton, 1974) 55.
13. *Ibid.*
14. Sidney Richman, *Bernard Malamud* (New York: Twayne, 1966) 33.
15. Bernard Malamud, *The Assistant* (Harmondsworth: Penguin, 1967) 30.
16. Ihab Hassan, *Radical Innocence: Studies in the Contemporary American Novel* (Princeton: Princeton Univ. Press, 1961) 11.
17. Philip Rahv, "A Note on Bernard Malamud," *Literature and the Sixth Sense* (Boston: Houghton Muffin, 1966) 280.
18. Bernard Malamud, *A New Life* (New York: Avon, 1980) 176.
19. William Barret, *Irrational Man: A Study of Existential Philosophy* (New York: Doubleday, 1958) 190.
20. Max Lerner, *America as a Civilization* (New York: Simon and Schuster, 1957) 812.
21. R.W.B. Lewis, *Recent Fiction: Literature* (Madras: VOC Forum Lecturers, 1971) 207.
22. *Ibid.*

23. Bernard Malamud, *The Fixer* (Harmondsworth: Penguin, 1967) 14.
24. Bernard Malamud, *The Tenants* (Harmondsworth: Penguin, 1971) 171.
25. Daniel Stern, "The Art of Fictional: Bernard Malamud," *The Paris Review*, 61 (1975) 47.
26. Morris Dickstein, "*The Tenants*," *New York Times Book Review* (October 3, 1971) 15.
27. Cynthia Ozick, "Literary Blacks and Jews" *Midstream*, 18 (1972) 20.
28. Morris Dickstein, 20.
29. Bernard Malamud, *Dubin's Lives* (Harmondsworth: Penguin, 1979) 18.
30. Sheldon J. Harshinow, 118.
31. Richard Gilman, *The New Republic* (March 24, 1979) 29.
32. Katha Pollitt, "Creator on Creating: Bernard Malamud," *Saturday Review*, 8 (1981) 38.
33. Bernard Malamud, *God's Grace* (Harmondsworth: Penguin, 1983) 82.
34. Joel Salzberg, *Critical Essays on Bernard Malamud* (Boston: G.K. Hall, 1987) 210
35. Alan Lelchuck, "Malamud's Dark Fable," *New York Times Book Review*, 87 (August 29,1982) 15.
36. Granville Hicks, "His Hope on the Human Heart," *Saturday Review* (October 12, 1963) 32.
37. *Ibid.*
38. Bernard Malamud, *The Magic Barrel* (Harmondsworth: Penguin, 1968) 9.
39. Bernard Malamud, *Idiots First* (New York: Farrar, Straus and Giroux, 1963) 6.
40. Sheldon J. Harshinow, 127.
41. Robert Solotaroff, *Bernard Malamud: A Study of the Short Fiction* (Boston; Twayne, 1989)70.
42. Marc L. Ratner, 670.
43. Jeffrey Helterman, *Understanding Bernard Malamud* (Caroline: Univ. of South Carolina, 1985) 80.
44. Tony Tanner, 322.
45. Lucio P. Ruolo, *Six Existential Heroes: The Politics of Faith* (Cambridge: Harvard Univ. Press, 1973)125.
46. Bernard Malamud, *Pictures of Fidelman: An Exhibition* (Harmondsworth: Penguin, 1972) 34.

47. Daniel Stern, 51.
48. Sheldon J. Harshinow, 86.
49. Bernard Malamud, *Rembrandt's Hat* (Harmondsworth: Penguin, 1973) 14.
50. Robert Solotaroff, 127.

# Exile and Alientation

Bernard Malamud in his novels is basically concerned with the afflicted, the imbalanced and disillusioned man groping for identity and recognition. In a world of shifting values, when novelists do not find a ready-made substructure of unquestioned religious, ethical, philosophical or even political varieties to shape their works, but are, on the contrary, faced with unanswered questions, perhaps the Jew writers, in their ancient role as introspective intellectuals, can give us "a truthful image of the moral anxiety haunting members of their generation."[1] Centuries of exile and alienation and untold suffering have elicited from the Jews a distinct response to the harsh realities of existence. In the process of their millennial martyrdom, suffering has evoked significant ethics of life which is as valuable to the present day world as it was to the Jews of the East-European ghettos. Rosenfled parallels one of the major problems of our times to that of the Jews:

> Alienation puts him [the Jew] in touch with his own past traditions, the history of Diaspora, with the present predicament of almost all intellectuals, and, for all one knows, with the future conditions of civilized humanity. Today, nearly all sensibility—thought, creation, perception—is in exile, alienated from society in which it barely managed to stay alive.[2]

Malamud has used the Jew as a representative of modern man, particularly as a symbol of hopefulness and self-identity in the face of suffering and isolation. He has discovered that this distinctly identifiable Jewish experience, when isolated and magnified, reflects the general human experience. He has asserted more than once that he was mythologizing the Jewish experience in his works. Malamud's Jews hardly share the religious, historical or sociological facts which generally identify the Jews.

The answer to why Malamud is so involved with man's 'devaluation and fragmentation' and with the problem of suffering lies in the philosophical climate of the twentieth century in which the currents of exile and alienation have invested the problem with a new relevance. This is not to say that Malamud is an existentialist writer; it is only to suggest that the existential mood has penetrated so deeply into the modern mind that if it is ultimately rejected it must be taken into account.

In the existential view, man's worth is determined by or consists solely of personality which can only be achieved through a painful process. The weak man acquiesces, the man with an existential sense of himself struggles and suffers. Maurice Friedman writes:

> Personality is suffering. The struggle to achieve personality and its consolidation are a painful process. The self-realization of personality presupposes resistance, it demands a conflict with the enslaving power of the world, a refusal to conform to the world. Refusal of personality acquiescence in dissolution in the surrounding world can lessen the suffering, and man easily goes that way. Acquiescence in slavery diminishes suffering, refusal increases it. Pain in the human world is the birth of personality, its fight for its own nature.[3]

For some of Malamud's characters, this struggle for their own nature is pain without issue; ultimately they fail. But for Roy Hobbes, Frank Alpine, S. Levin, Yakov Bok and Harry Lesser there is a sense in which they achieve themselves through suffering, in acceptance of themselves in their anguished existential condition. The value of suffering lies in coming to know the 'I' in answering 'who am I'? for "only [man's] suffering and his satisfactions instruct him concerning himself."[4]

Malamud's protagonist, termed as the "confessional hero"[5] by Peter Axthelm, is vitally concerned with intellectual and spiritual questions, and, since he is passionately involved with discovering his own nature, he always suffers: "He [confessional hero] views his condition not with anger but with deep internal pain; he rejects external rebellion in favour of self-laceration. His suffering originates not in the chaos of the world but in the chaos within the self and for him the only possible order or value must be found in self-understanding."[6]

Malamud speaks for those who are seeking, through a maze of social and philosophical blind alleys, for reattainment of self. In his novels, the problem of personal suffering is particularly relevant for where the hero carries his personal existence in its total weight.

We live in an age in which the nature of guilt and punishment, anxiety and suffering are understood in a context resulting ultimately from the Freudian psychology. One cannot understand Roy Hobbes, Frank Alpine, S. Levin, Yakov Bok and Harry Lesser or others if one cannot accept the underlying assumptions. Freud says that suffering threatens us from three directions: "from our own body which is doomed to decay and dissolution and which cannot even do without pain and anxiety as warning signals; from the external world, which may rage against us with overwhelming and merciless forces of destruction; and, finally from our relations to other men. The suffering which comes from this last source is perhaps more painful to us than any more."[7]

Malamud's protagonists usually suffer from dissatisfaction with their present condition, and after a period of suffering, depending on their capacity to learn and arrive at a greater measure of self-understanding. The success in their quest for identity depends on their appreciation of the value of suffering as a means of asserting their humanity and acceptance of responsibility for others. Most of Malamud's heroes start as self-exiles; their struggle to seek re-integration with the self from which they are alienated sometimes is successful and sometimes it isn't. Theodore Solotaroff points out: "Malamud's chief figures are confronted less by the world than by themselves."[8] The opposition of the part that judges and the part that does things implies alienation and the progress of Malamud's fragmented figures is often measured by the degree of integration they achieve with the self. The self-confrontation is frequently the result of a spiritual or moral crisis initiated by their dialogue with the other.

Malamud's first novel *The Natural* is quite different in both subject and treatment from his later fictions. It has, for instance, no specifically Jewish content. Indeed, Malamud has moved into a world where, Sandy Koufax notwithstanding, the Jew has usually been conspicuous by his absence, the world of big league baseball. However, Malamud is merely trimming with allusion and myth the basic ingredient out of which he will concoct all the later novels. His concerns in *The Natural*, as in all his fiction, are with the *Schlemiel* hero, the eternal victim overtaken by fate, morality and the meaning of suffering in a man's life. "Roy Hobbs serves as archetype for all of Malamud's small heroes, who . . . fall victim to a tragic flaw aggravated by misfortune."[9]

Roy's encounter with Harriet Bird causes him to suffer for fifteen years, thus postponing his ambition for a considerable period. In the second part "Batter Up!" we meet Roy trying to pull himself out of obscurity and loneliness. He still wants to realize the dream that was shattered with a silver bullet; he is ambitious to be a record-breaker, for he feels, "If you leave all those record that nobody else can beat—they'll always remember you. You sorta (sic) never die."[10] At nineteen he was a 'natural' with a talent to hit the top in the baseball world. At thirty-four, with fifteen years of hardships behind him, he is a 'disciplined quester' for the glory he could have naturally got at nineteen had Harriet not shot him for his *hubris*.

Often, in Malamud's fiction the conflict within the protagonist's mind is externalized through the device of the double or the second self. Another person becomes the symbol of the protagonist's own divided self.

> When an author portrays a protagonist as seeing his double, it is not simply a device or a gimmick calculated to arouse the reader's interest by virtue of the strangeness of the episode, but is, in fact, the result of his sense of the division to which the human mind in conflict with itself is susceptible.[11]

In the 'Pre-game,' Harriet Bird is Roy's mirror image. She, because of her superior knowledge of the need to lead a more meaningful life, acts as his conscience. She helps Roy confront the dualities within himself, demanding he aspires for more meaningful goals in contrast to his egoistic desire to be the best baseball player. Her attempt to shoot Roy is symbolic of an affront to "kill" the narcissistic self-loving Roy. Roy does not die and even after fifteen years, he is still not free of his egoistic desires. Such self-preoccupation is morbid by Malamud's moral standards and undoubtedly self-destructive. It leads to much suffering. Roy will repeatedly suffer setbacks till he eventually learns to change his priorities.

Harriet's act of destruction is, in fact, "inwardly constructive."[12] She seeks to help Roy in his moral growth, "the point of the relationship between them is the adventure of the first self, the expanding of the horizon, the second self serving as the hammer to beat the metal of first into new shape."[13] Roy possesses the mythic generative qualities of heroes like Achilles and Sir Percival. However, "Roy has no comprehension of his role in the moral battle; he does not even recognize that such a cosmic struggle exists. He can think only of himself—his own glory, his own ambitions, his own physical desires."[14] It is his lack of moral awareness that leads to his failure twice over. Roy has already faced his fate once in the shape of the beautiful goddess Harriet who shot him for his self-serving desires. But he has learnt nothing from his past experiences and therefore will have to face his fate again. He will have to go through the trial of suffering again till he realizes his mistakes and learns from them.

Roy is discontented with his unhappy fate and not credulous when Iris tries to explain that experience makes people better through their suffering, "we have two lives, Roy, the life we learn with and the life we live with after that. Suffering is what brings us toward happiness," (48) tells Iris. Roy does not pay much heed to Iris's moralizing because he wilfully refuses to be convinced. "When will you grow up, Roy?" Iris despairs (206). He does not realize that suffering is an expression of onehood with others—the shaping of the others' fate thus lessening their burden. For Malamud, "suffering is a precondition of existence, the one possible mode of goodness and engagement in this world. One must suffer if one is to preserve one's integrity."[15] Roy's denial of his past experiences and sufferings is, in a way, a denial of himself. Suffering has never taught him to want the right things. "I have knocked around a lot and been hard in plenty of ways," he said huskily, ". . . but all that is gone now. I know I have the stuff and will get there . . . where I will be the champ and what goes with it," (114)—meaning wealth and fame.

At the end we see Roy walk in the street in lonely torture, feeling acutely sensitive to the wretchedness with which he has lived his live. He feels "overwhelming self-hatred. In each striking wave of it, he remembered some disgusting happening of his life" (222) and further broods over that, "I never did learn anything out of my past life, now I have to suffer again" (222). He is again plunged into suffering and humiliation because of his misdoing, "his thoughts were dismal. That frightened feeling: bust before beginning. On the merry-go-round again about his failure" (184).

However, although Roy has to face defeat in his earthly dreams, he wins a moral victory for he has realized his own mistakes. It is through a painful process of wavering between conflicting demands within himself that Roy ultimately reaches self-awareness. It is through the trial of suffering that he learns to place another above self. Having gained self-knowledge, Roy will be able to direct his life better than before. "The healing growth of the soul," C.P. Keppler says, is possible by "coming to know and accept and assimilate elements of the psyche of which one is not consciously aware, but by the emotional pressures of which one is strongly affected."[16] He faces up to the fact that he has never learnt anything from his past experiences. He grows up in his understanding of his predicament. "He wished he had no ambitions—often wondered where they had come from in his life, because he remembered how satisfied he has been as a youngster," (111) thinks Roy. This in itself is a mirror point but a major first step on the road to a better self. Though he does not actually experience rebirth, there is an unquestionable, positive sign of renewed self. The old self undergoes a symbolic death when Roy feels hatred for the self. Roy makes a moral affirmation when he accepts his fate. His life in the future will be no bed of roses but he will probably be more capable of facing whatever lies ahead of him for he has learnt to accept suffering as a necessary ingredient of life. Nor will he be a novice as he was before.

Similarly in his next novel, *The Assistant*, Malamud depicts the transformation of Frank Alpine from an alienated and undisciplined self to a morally integrated one through suffering. Frank's struggle for recognition takes the shape of his search for redemption through suffering. In the figure of Frank Alpine, the imperatives of suffering and the acceptance of responsibility as the means to the attainment of authenticity and identity are brought into clearer focus. In material terms, there is little change in the condition of Frank from the beginning to the end of the novel, yet at the end, he emerges as an individual with a moral code evolved out of his suffering. This is accomplished through his intimate acquaintance with the Hasidic personality of Morris Bober, as also through the suffering caused by his relationship with Morris's daughter Helen.

Morris Bober is a Jew living in a non-Jewish area. The Bobers, Karps and Pearls make up a small Jewish segment of the gentile community. However, even the Jews are alienated from each other. They share attached houses and stores but otherwise live in detachment. Bober's isolation is inescapable. What can he have in common with his neighbours? Unlike them he is not a commercial success, and unlike them he is obdurately honest. So he remains shut up in his store, keeping down contact with the outside to the minimum. Frank comments on this isolation:

> What kind of a man did you have to be born to shut yourself up in over-grown coffin and never once during the day, so help you, outside of going for your Yiddish Newspaper, poke you beak out of the door for a snootful of air? The answer wasn't hard to say—you had to be a Jew.[17]

Bober's daughter Helen remembers the time when her father would close the store, at least on Jewish holidays, and take family visiting or to see a Yiddish play. After the death of the son, Ephraim, however, Bober rarely went beyond the corner. The encapsulation of Bober's life is reinforced by description of the store as 'prison' and 'tomb.'

Frank Alpine gradually understands and adopts the Jewish ethic of suffering as exemplified by Morris Bober. In his first appearance in the novel, Frank is an accomplice to Ward Minogue and holds up the poor Jewish storekeeper. Later, a desire to atone for the act of hate against Bober propels Frank back to the store. It is his relationship with Bober which assists him to an understanding of what it means to suffer. At first there is a contradiction in their attitudes towards suffering. While Frank is repelled by suffering, Bober believes that he must suffer for some goodness. Sacrifice and suffering are more important to him than the observance of holy days and the rules of Kosher:

> This is not important to me if I taste pig or I don't. To some Jews this is important but not to me. Nobody will tell me that I am not Jewish because I put in my mouth once in a while, when my tongue is dry, a piece of ham. But they will tell me and I will believe them, if I forget the Law. This means to other people. Our life is hard enough. Why should he hurt somebody else? (122)

It is this ethic that impels Bober to give credit to a drunk woman even though there is no guarantee of payment, or to wake up every morning for the poor old "Polisheh" who buys one roll from him for three cents, or to run two blocks in the snow, without rubbers to protect his feet, to give back five-cents that a poor Italian lady forgot on the counter, Bober knows the value of sympathy and sacrifice. He teaches Frank the ancient wisdom, "If you live you suffer. . . . I suffer for you . . . you suffer for me." (113)

At first, Frank is repelled by Bober's ethic of self-denial and sacrifice and his calm acceptance of suffering:

> That's what they live for, Frank thought, to suffer. And the one that got the biggest pain in the gut and can hold on to it the longest is the best Jew. No wonder they got on his nerves. (81)

Frank is initially revolted by the Jewish attitude to suffering, but gradually he attains an understanding of it. The change and development in his viewpoint first makes itself felt in his conversation with Helen. When she tells him, "Frank sometimes things turn out other than we plan. Do not feel hurt," and Frank declares, "When I don't feel hurt, I hope they bury me" (81). He has arrived at an understanding of the fact that 'if you live you suffer.'

Gradually Frank realizes that importance of suffering for others. Initially he had experienced "a craving that somebody suffer as his own fortune improved" (84). In contrast to his earlier attitude, he now learns to identify himself with others. He takes over responsibility for the store and shares in the poverty and frustration of the Bobers. The end of the novel is exactly like the beginning, except Frank has replaced Bober. Without caring about his own fortunes, Frank chooses to share the "squalor and sickening destitution of the Bobers" in the "blood-sucking store." His association with Bober has taught him the value of suffering for some earthly good. Frank Alpine now embraces the Jewish ethic of suffering for some fundamental goodness. At the end of the novel, Frank has himself circumcised. "The pain enraged and inspired him. After Passover, he became a Jew" (217). In *The Assistant*, Malamud demonstrates that the suffering for the hero is spiritually edifying. It confers on a human being the inestimate boon of a meaningful life. At the end of the novel Frank Alpine's life is wretched, but his misery and suffering have their own spiritual rewards. He is a better man, capable of sympathy and concern for others, even at the cost of his own hopes and ambitions.

The physical pain of the circumcision is merely an external manifestation of a new excruciating suffering. That the suffering he comprehends and accepts is not Jewish in the theological sense of the term but of a general nature, is implicit in the fact that Morris Bober is not an orthodox Jew, for he does not obey Mosaic dietary laws, nor does he regularly attend religious services; he is a Jew in that he is "in exile, exiled from most of his own formal traditions."[18] In his final conversion to Judaism, Frank "eradicates the barriers between theologies,"[19] and emerges as a suffering man. Frank's sense of equilibrium in suffering is the most affirmative sense of identity.

In *A New Life*, Malamud has removed his *schlemiel* hero from the ghettoized New York of *The Assistant* across the continent to Cascadia College. S. Levin the hero of *A New Life* is also alienated, though there is nothing peculiarly Jewish about his isolation. Levin is no stranger to suffering when he arrives at Cascadia. He enters the scene on the first page of the novel, "trailing visible clouds of glory from a past of the most unmitigated suffering."[20] His father was a thief who died in prison, his mother a mad woman who killed herself with a bread knife. Mourning them as well as a woman he loved who had cast him aside, Levin became a drunk, living a hopeless derelict life until in a moment of revelation in someone's filthy cellar he awoke to the realization "that life is holy. I then became a man of principle."[21]

The novel *A New Life* offers the possibility of human salvation and realization of identity through "a consciously constructed personal ethic."[22] S. Levin discovers this personal ethic and is redeemed. He is redeemed by his sufferings: purgatorial fires have refined him during his search for self-discipline, and a new meaningful life directed by humanistic values. An underground man yearning for a 'new life,' Levin is a humanist; but he is also a man of principles out of touch with principles. Like Morris, the sad-faced Levin is a man who "creates his own peril" (58) and for his ceaseless yearning to connect with life, he must suffer the indignity of abrupt reversals. Malamud has discovered a more pervasive frame in this novel in order to demonstrate his theme of "suffering and regeneration."[23]

*A New Life* is mainly a study in the difficulties of undoing the hold of a deprived and wasted past, of breaking "through the hardened cement of self-frustration,"[24] to freedom and control. Malamud's protagonists have or gain deep knowledge of suffering, whether in the flesh from poverty and illness or in mind from frustration and remorse. S. Levin's suffering ensues from his relationship with Pauline Gilley and Gerald Gilley. Levin rebels against Gerald Gilley, the director of composition and ultimately replaces him. Levin has a sense of disparity between the values cherished by him and those of Gerald Gilley from the very beginning and this provides a clue to the ultimate conflict between them. Gilley is hearty, unintrospective and does not share Levin's enthusiasm for the liberal arts. Levin, on the other hand, is the liberal dreamer, the enthusiast of the American Dream, while Gilley with his anti-intellectualism is a "representative of the mechanistic, anti-humanistic tone of the college."[25] Levin senses a threat to his integrity when he comes to suspect that Gilley had given him the job to ensure himself of Levin's support in a possible election for the chairmanship of the department.

This conflict between Gilley's conservatism and Levin's untested faith in liberal values comes to the surface very early and is the source of friction between them. While Levin is an idealist, Gilley is a materialist. As against Levin's anxiety to establish himself at Cascadia College, the predestined direction of his movement is prophesized in his installation in the room formerly occupied by an instructor Leo Duffy. Like Duffy before him, Levin is a champion of the liberal arts, "whose one purpose is to upset other people's apple cart" (203). His career at Cascadia College is in some respects a re-enactment of Duffy's career. As he had replaced Gilley, so he did with Duffy. Levin gains knowledge of suffering by replacing them which can help him achieve his identity in the new environment.

Levin seeks spiritual rebirth in the corrupt milieu of Cascadia College and as a strategy for survival attempts to avoid involvement with faculty wives and girl students. But his unsatisfied need for community makes him seek fellowship which he can find only in Gerald Gilley, while Fabricant and Bockett hardly respond to his overtures of friendship. From Levin's point of view, the members of the department fall in two groups: the materialist comprising Gilley and his supporters Avis Fliss and George Bullock; the liberals comprising Fabricant, Joe Bockett and others. Almost against his will, Levin becomes a sympathizer of Fabricant. He is antagonized by Gilley's ill-concealed anxiety to please a comparative newcomer like him by giving a separate room and making him the chairman of the text book committee. He feels his integrity challenged by these efforts of Gilley to 'buy' his support in the event of a departmental election. Despite his intentions to abide by the rules, Levin almost compulsively clashes with Gilley, first over a cribbed paper submitted by a student in Levin's class, and then over a textbook containing an alleged indecent story by Hemingway. As the novel progresses, Levin "assumes the ironic consciousness that challenges the values around him."[26] He is unable to adjust to the mechanical routine of the English department and little on the fostering of human values among the students. Levin's failure to identify the source of the apparently cribbed paper exposes him to the scorn both of Gilley and the students. It is a testimony to Levin's humanity that he is moved by the student's harassed look and feels that Albert Bridless, the student, "had got to where his guilt, by some trick of human drama rubbed off on his persecutors" (91). Unmindful of the possible consequence of his action, Levin gives up the search and confesses his failure to the student. Levin, indeed, epitomizes the modern man's condition—struggling, stumbling ahead, not winning, but not losing either. In his condition suffering is as blindly apparent as the winter sun on a snowy field. Levin is Malamud's *Schlemiel* who exposes himself continuously to rebuffs, absurdities and humiliations.

The fact that Levin, an Easterner, comes to the West, and that he is an outsider accentuates his isolation. Levin's quest for emotional identity and, to reduce his isolation, is full of incidents which brings out comic ineptitude and innate integrity which does not permit him to compromise. The weakness of his will is brought out in his fleeting affair with his student Nadalee. He tries to adhere to his resolve in the face of her provocative conduct, but finally yields to her invitation to spend a weekend with her in a motel on the coast. The affair which gives him more anxiety than pleasure appears to justify his words to Gilley: "I get shocked when I try to get away with something" (91). This source of Levin's anxiety is identified by Sidney Richman when he says that though Levin has more insight than Frank Alpine, "he is still Levin at war with the morality which defines his nature."[27]

Levin's relationship with Pauline Gilley brings into focus his conscious quest for social identity as a teacher, and his latent quest for emotional identity. Levin's affair with Pauline wavers between mutual attraction and separation resulting from ambivalent motives. Both want a fuller life but are unwilling to endanger their present state of relative security. Like Helen, Pauline does not recognize that Levin is her "man of possibilities" (176), neither feels a commitment to other. Levin's spiritual development is also faltering, for he knows that his redemption lies in emotional identity but finds himself incapable of commitments. His device of evasion and self-justification such as telling himself that the Gilleys are indifferent to each other, and invoking his resentment against Gilley for transferring students from his class without informing him, fail to conceal from him the gulf between his ideals and actions. The decision to accept commitment as the sole means of attaining identity is long in the making in Levin's mind. He tries to convince himself that he is not responsible for Pauline by arguing that she had been in search of adventure only. He thinks that he might even turn out to be benefactor of the Gilleys if the affair reactivates their attraction or alternatively that, "he could break if off by spending the summer in San Francisco" (183). But these answers do not allow Levin to evade for long the central question of the choice between isolation and commitment. The emotional turmoil caused by the moral conflict manifests itself somatically in Levin as "a fiery pain in the batt" (185). After much psychological resistance and self-denial, Levin has the insight that his attempted isolation had been the cause of his condition. This realization clears the way for his progress towards his attainment of authenticity and acceptance.

Levin's predicament regarding the choice between detachment and commitment is reflected in his reaction to an apparent break in his affair with Pauline. When out of mingled feeling of guilt and love for Gerald, Pauline stops seeing him, Levin tries to feel relief at the removal of the threat to his security in the College. But his desire for her allows him no rest until he renews his guilty relationship with her. Though Levin has sensual feeling but his concept of emotional identity gains a broader spectrum. This progressive refinement of Levin's self is a discontinuous process, the experiences themselves being "conceived as occurring in an endless moment to moment discontinuity."[28] The process is further obscured by his agony and introspection. The awakened moral self of Levin makes him consider the emotional strain their relation imposes on Pauline and makes him give her up. Levin's integrity manifests itself in this act of renunciation when he learns of Pauline's relation with Duffy and feels embittered with her. This new knowledge makes renunciation easier and more painless for him reducing his sense of guilt at his leaving her.

The fits of despondency in Levin are a part of the pattern of the Malamudian hero's quest and are distinctly reminiscent of Frank Alpine's introspection and despair. Richman says that Levin differs from Frank and Morris, "neither in his intellect nor in his ideals—but rather in the energy with which he seeks connections with this world."[29] But Levin does differ from the earlier heroes in the intellectual clarity with which he defines his goals and apprehends the forces thwarting his quest. Though the difference is not so much qualitative as quantitative, it is unmistakably clear and important. While Frank Alpine blamed himself for his failure, Levin blames Pauline and does not admit his own responsibility. But this dense cloud of defeatist thinking and self-recrimination obscures Levin's progress towards the attainment and the growth of his moral consciousness. At the end of this period of agony, he emerges with a balanced vision, capable of doing justice to Pauline in his thoughts. Like Frank Alpine who embraces Judaism, Levin accepts Pauline and achieves his heroism by "willingly taking a lead of family commitments."[30] He accepts Pauline as well as her adopted children, knowing well the problems they entail.

Levin's heroism is of a natural kind; it is that of the ordinary unheroic man. He is "neither a mythical folk hero nor a saint but a coward who suffers and triumphs albeit ambigously!"[31] He accepts the burden of supporting a family without any job, simply because as he says to Gerald, "I can" (292). His triumph is, however, equivocal, for he learns that it was Pauline who had chosen him for the job and that the choice was the outcome of fortuitous resemblance to Leo Duffy, who also had a beard. He is thus true, as Weiss says, to the Dostoevskian cult of suffering and martyrdom.

Levin's suffering originates from his taking responsibility for others. In his exit, at the end, from the college, Levin has transcended Duffy's destiny. His going out into the world with a crushing burden of commitments without any promise of a job, mirrors the precariousness of existential man's predicament. Levin gains an insight into the meaning of suffering and emerges with an identity defined by his commitment to responsibility for others.

In *The Fixer*, Malamud seems to have deserted the modern world for the world of Yiddish fiction. His locale has shifted from modern urban America to early twentieth-century Russia, the world of the Pale, of progress, and tea-drinking old man in caftans who approach the problem of life through the medieval structure of a religion whose tenants govern their every waking moment. The hero, Yakov Bok, is the *Shtetl* handyman, building and finishing furniture, painting, plastering, doing all the odd jobs which more educated Jews shun.

But the novel is modern not only in technique but in theme; the Yiddish atmosphere, the East European flavour, is merely background for a stark modern fable about Jews caught in the vise of history, about alienated man and his re-integration into society, his re-absorption into humanity. It is a novel which focuses with excruciating intensity on one man's suffering and the profound changes which occur as that suffering strips away the inmost reaches of self, opening its victim to knowledge.

*The Fixer* is based on the notorious case of Mendal Beiliss, a Jew, falsely accused of the ritual murder of a young Christian boy in Kiev in 1913. Of course, the novel is not a case study as it has been pointed out by some critics because Malamud throws light on his intention:

> I want to say this about *The Fixer*. The story of Yakov Bok, the fixer, is an imaginative piece of work . . . you can't make a thing more real than it is but you can make it seem more real through the imaginative fact. . . . You see for me, the book has a mythological

> quality. It has to be treated as a myth, an endless story, more than a case study. A case study couldn't be art.[32]

Yakov Bok is made the victim of anti-Semitic hate and fury in the Tsarist Russia. He is subjected to incredible torture and suffering in a Tsarist prison cell. The suffering heaped on Yakov Bok is undoubtedly hair-raising, but it does not take its origin from perverse sense of pleasure on the part of the author in inflicting torture on Bok. The suffering that Bok undergoes is meaningful and spiritually rewarding. Yakov Bok grows in stature and the horrors of his imprisonment became the source of his moral regeneration. Malamud draws attention to this when he says: "Yakov had a lot to learn and maybe he learned it. His experience in prison leads to a change in him that is the drama of the book."[33] In fact, Bok is aware of this change and says, "I'm not the same man I was."[34]

In the beginning of the novel Yakov Bok is contrasted with his kind and forgiving father-in-law. Shmuel "sucked tea through sugar but his son-in-law drank his unsweetened. It tasted bitter and he blamed existence" (9). It is a telling description of the kind of man Bok is: harsh and embittered. Bok bitterly recounts his misfortunes to Samuel: "I've been cheated from the start," (10) he cries. Yakov blames his wife for not having borne him a child. He stops sleeping with her and when she runs away from him, he curses her vehemently. His father-in-law tries to evoke sympathy in Yakov by reminding him how the childless Raisl had run frantically to rabbis and doctors, and had finally run away in desperation. Yakov only says mercilessly: "May she run forever" (11).

Yakov Bok is obviously a selfish, dissatisfied and uncharitable man. His whole life is unpleasant to him, and he has a strong sense of being imprisoned, which he attributes to the stifling conditions of the *Shtetl*. An embittered and selfish man to begin with, Bok gradually accepts the ethical datum of human responsibility and love. Shmuel first points to the chief flaw in Bok's character—his lack of charity: "'Charity you were always short of,' the peddler said. Yakov rose enraged, 'Don't talk to me about charity. . . . Because I have no charity to give'." (11)

Through his experience in prison, however, Bok learns to be a kinder and more compassionate man. This transformation is reflected in the change of his attitude towards his wife. At first, provoked by her elopement, Bok assumes a harsh and self-righteous attitude towards her. This attitude is gradually modified so that Bok becomes more sympathetic and forgiving.

Love and sympathy replace Bok's earlier hard indifference towards his wife. When she visits him in prison, he is able to say:

> I'm sorry I stopped sleeping with you. I was out to stab myself, so I stabbed you. Who else was so close to me? Still I've suffered in this prison and I am not the same human I once was. What more can I say Raisl? If I had my life to live over, you'd have leto cry about, so stop crying. (259)

In an outstanding act of benevolence, Yakov Bok declares himself father of Chaim, his wife's illegitimate son. He is no longer the selfish and callous man he had once been.

Bok's moral enlargement is even more conspicuously evident in his relationship with the Jewish community. He moves from a stifling pre-occupation with himself to concern and involvement with the Jews and, ultimately, to all mankind. In the beginning, Bok refused to identify himself with the Jewish community. According to him, being a Jew is an "everlasting curse" (216). He declares vehemently that he is "sick of their history, destiny blood-guilt" (207). Bok alienates himself from the community, and tries to obliterate any identification with it. However, three years of dark and dismal imprisonment teach him to view the history, destiny and blood-guilt of the Jews with a different attitude. The anti-Semitic fury directed against him propels him to a closer identification with the Jewish people. He realizes that his fate is inextricably linked with that of his people, that "there is no way of keeping the consequences of his death to himself" (240). Bok pleads himself to the cause of the Jews: "He will protect them to the extent that he can. This is his covenant with himself" (245). Yakov refuses to accept a pardon and demands a trial by jury, not for fear that a confession will 'doom him forever' but out of enlarged human sympathy and concern for the community. He acquires the dimensions of a willing sufferer in the cause of the Jews.

Thus, although Bok himself denies the educational values of suffering when he says, "what suffering has taught me is the uselessness of suffering" (298), it has been the cause of his moral regeneration. Suffering has made him identify with family, his community and ultimately with all mankind. It has been the source of an enlarged human sympathy and concern which rescues Bok from his earlier selfishness and lack of charity, and grants him the boon of sel m .Uf-transcendence.

In *The Tenants*, Malamud returns to his familiar terrain of gloomy, wasted New York streets and shows the forces of fragmentation and alienation that demoralize our lives. Its protagonist, Harry Lesser, the Jewish writer is a *Schlemiel* who turns back to the distinct past and contemplates the futility of life. He broods over his orphan life: "Death of his mother in a street accident when he was kid. . . . Death of his older brother in the war. . . . Life so fragile, fleeting. An aged father he hasn't seen in years."[35] Lesser is an alienated individual living in a prison of his own making. Like the Wastelanders confirming their own prisoners, Lesser confirms his prison by constant denial to any change. He is like the Wastelanders who "think of the key, each in prison/thinking of the key, each confirms a prison."[36] The prison of tenement becomes a metaphor for the human predicament. Malamud has commented:

> Perhaps I see it has a metaphor for dilemma of all men: necessity, whose bars we look through and try to see, social injustice, apathy, and ignorance. The personal prison of entrapment in past experience, guilt, obsession . . . the somewhat blind or blinded self, in other words.[37]

Inevitably Harry Lesser appears to be moving towards the state of self-exile. He almost buries himself in the apartment: "Only when inside his safe and save three rooms Lesser felt himself close off the world and relax" (16). Lesser's involvement with writing keeps him off from the world, as he says: "He would not think how much of life he made no attempt to use. That was outside and he was in" (16). The tenement provides an image of death and desolation. Lesser once hears 'mournful wind' and graveyard music, and suspects funeral parlour on the premises. He thinks each book he writes nudges him that much 'close to death' and not life.

Lesser is less than human in his response to the repeated pleas of his landlord, Irving Levenspiel. As a statutory tenant he refuses to leave the tenement till the completion of his unfinished novel. Levenspiel has his own domestic problems and craves for the mercy of Lesser. The landlord emerges as a symbolic reminder of life and its values which Lesser disregards. Lesser betrays a total lack of compassion. He refuses Levenspiel's offer of bribe and involves him in a prolonged legal battle. He is worried only about his future as a writer. Levenspiel wishes Lesser were 'a less egotistical type' to realize other's predicament. He tries unsuccessfully to break Lesser's shell of egotism with his sarcastic remarks: "For Christ's sake, what are you writing, the Holy Bible?" (22) But Lesser does not understand the value of heart.

Lesser finds his kin in Willie Spearmint, the black writer, who also chooses the same desolate tenement in his search for a private place to do his writing. One day Lesser discovers Willie in his flat seriously typing. His first thought was to devise a means to get rid of him. Willie's response to Lesser is also very sullen. He complains: "Man . . . can't you see me writing my book?" (27). When Lesser apologetically says, "I'm a writer myself," he just stares at him. The gulf between the two writers is suggested in Willie's lack of response to Lesser's outstretched hand for a shake.

While Lesser's writing reveals psychological tensions, Willie's work characterizes a revolutionary outburst of black anger. The soul of Willie is in his writing. Willie who was imprisoned for sometime by the whites, feels that he will be the 'best soul writer' by writing about "the terrible and violent things of my life" (32). It eases his self. The violence shows Willie's 'unspent rage.' Unlike Lesser, Willie has amelioristic aim of the sociological approach to literature. He believes that he can help his people overthrow racism and economic equality through writing. He wants to "make black more than color or culture, and outrage larger than protest or ideology" (54). Lesser is moved by 'the affecting' subject of Willie's work and his attempt to define himself and his sense of suffering and injustice. But he finds Willie woefully lacking the craft of writing. Emotion overpowers technique. While Lesser's craft outweighs his theme, Willie's powerful theme betrays poor treatment.

The first sign of disharmony between Lesser and Willie comes out with Lesser's genuine criticism of Willie's manuscript. Lesser points out that black experience cannot become literature "just by writing it down" (60). Willie who is deeply prejudiced against white fails to accept Lesser's criticism in right spirit. He considers Lesser unfit to judge the black experience as he is white.

Both Lesser and Willie feel 'mutually repelled' when they meet one winter night on the frigid stairs. They, however, seem to forgive each other. Yet the black is not free from his prejudice against the Jews. Lesser's exhortation for peace fails on Willie. Willie is sore that on account of Lesser, he "can't write the way I used to any more" (169). Lesser out of frustration in his work destroys Willie's typewriter and thinks that the writing might go well thereafter, but it does not. He vainly hopes he could write after the exit of Willie from the house. The final ending of the novel shows Lesser and Willie bloodthirsty. One moonless night, they meet near a bush and kill each other.

The last sentence, "Each, thought the writer, feels the anguish of the other" (173) reveals that it is a fantasy. It may be inferred from the sentence that both of them would feel the anguish of the other at least at the time of their death. Feeling anguish of the other is one's capacity for compassion and understanding. Lesser thus emerges out of the tragic encounter with a new insight. "Here is suggested a sort of limited 'redemption'; it implies a recognition of 'the other' and an insight into his anguish."[38]

Bernard Malamud tells Daniel Stern: "In my books I go along the seem paths in different worlds."[39] If one were to delve deep into his novel *Dubin's Lives*, the process of self-education could easily be gauged. Primarily it presents the crisis-ridden marital life of William B. Dubin. Despite moving in a startlingly new direction in this book, Malamud's focus on life remains undeflected. The protagonist's recollection of his father reminds us of Morris Bober; his struggle with the current book parallels Harry Lesser's despair with words and ideas and the pastoral love-scene re-enacts the erotic union between Levin and Pauline in *A New Life*. Besides, Dubin's affair with the young girl Fanny Bick in *Dubin's Lives* suggests a recurring motif in Malamud's writing: man's initially succumbing to temptation and later realizing his folly, ultimately discovering the gap between transient pleasure and enduring satisfaction.

When the novel opens, Dubin, the biographer, is fifty-six, living in Camp Campobello on the New York-Vermont border. Married to Kitty for twenty-five years, he has problems with his new book, the biography of D.H. Lawrence. Dubin and Kitty have two children—Gerald from Kitty's earlier marriage, and Maud, a student at Berkeley. Later Maud joins a Buddhist commune and carries an affair with a black professor, a little older than Dubin. Despite Kitty's depression and eloquent references to her dead husband, she and Dubin make a relatively happy couple. When Fanny Bick, twenty-two, a little older than Maud, enters their house as a 'cleaning person,' Dubin's struggle with the book get further aggravated. After his initial attempt to resist the 'dark force of blood consciousness,' he gets romantically attached to Fanny. In order to experience 'plenitude of life through love,' Dubin and Fanny fly to Venice where the erotic mission ends in a fiasco. On return, Dubin suffers a long winter of self-accusation and creative failure. He starts making a headway with the biography when Fanny again appears on the scene. The two often meet in New York, and later in Dubin's barn study. When she wants Dubin to choose between her and Kitty, he ingeniously proposes an adjustment that each week he would spend a few days with her and other with his wife. When the novel closes, Dubin is still divided between his feverish attachment to the girl and a tender concern for his wife. Whereas with Fanny he feels to be sexually adequate, with his wife of fifty-one years he fears he is growing impotent.

In Dubin we see the contradictions that are essentially a part of the human character. We note "double-edged nature of Dubin's search for a new life, a search bounded on one side by the yearning to experience the fullness of life in all its sensuality, vitality and freedom: on the other by self-deception."[40] In him we see "the struggle to accommodate warring (or, at least, contending) impulses and desire to negotiate some kind of inner peace of balance of power, or perhaps just to maintain hostilities at a low destructive level, between . . . the impeccable, singular lusts for the flesh and its pleasures. The measured self vs. the insatiable self, the accommodating self vs. the ravenous self."[41] As Dubin's affair with Fanny flourishes and blooms one gets the feeling that Dubin has escaped the pressures of conformism which binds Malamud's former heroes. But we might have guessed that "sex untainted by guilt and the merciless stab of conscience, the uninhibited liberty to seek out the lineament of gratified desire wherever or however he chooses"[42] can never be the good fortune of a Malamudian hero, not even for Dubin, however unorthodox a Malamud hero he may be.

Shades of the old Malamud appear now and then. Knowing rules by now, one can anticipate the outcome of the Venice episode. A series of comic tragedies overtake Dubin. Fanny suffers from diarrohoea after eating a dish of brains. Dubin spends holiday doctoring her. When she is better and Dubin looks forward to consummation, he finds her on the floor making love to an ardent gondolier. He is made out to be a characteristic Malamudian character—a *Schlemiel*. He cannot enjoy fulfilment of carnal appetite without paying for it by way of purgative suffering. "Just as nothing succeeds like failure in earlier Malamud books, nothing fails like success"[43] in *Dubin's Lives*. His troubles increase in proportion to his youthful pleasures and for his breaches Dubin pays heavily as retribution: "One paid for the pursuit of youth—from Faustus to Wm. Dubin."[44]

Dubin and Fanny take full pleasure in each other but, nonetheless, Dubin suffers from the familiar pangs of conscience. An orthodox Synagogue overlooks their love-nest and the rabbi praying at the window reminds Dubin of his forsaken duties towards his wife. He is both libidinous and obsessively guilty. "The secret escapist urge to remain uninvolved with life competes with the call (often prompted by guilt) to a conscious and willed acceptance of responsibility."[45] Placed in an uncompromising situation with incompatible dualities of marriage and extra-marital affair, emotion and reason, Kitty and Fanny Dubin is compelled to define his choice.

The alienation in Dubin's life is not simply the outcome of his affair with Fanny. Dubin is a narcissist, so absorbed in himself that one is surprised at his interest in Fanny. Dubin enters into the affair with Fanny wholeheartedly but suffers much because of the confusion it creates in his orderly life. His desire for the affair comes into conflict with his self-hatred for having begun it. The effort to keep it a secret makes him think, "one may be able to mask dishonesty but not its effects" (256). His marriage, his work, his mental and physical powers all seem to disintegrate in the face of his quest for a new life of self-fulfilment. Malamud has said, "One must accept limits on one's needs in order to live effectively with others, so that the gift of life may function."[46] This is the lesson all Malamud's protagonists learn through a painful process and this is what Dubin will also learn slowly and painfully. By learning to strike a balance between his own conflicting selves Dubin will find acceptance and authenticity in life.

From Dubin, the biographer, Malamud goes to Calvin Cohn, the paleologist in his last novel *God's Grace*. Malamud describes in this novel in a primitivistic setting the desperate efforts of lonely Cohn to achieve a sense of community with the animals as well. The emphasis on the need of compassion becomes markedly explicit in the novel. Indeed, in this novel Malamud makes an effort to protect civilization from self-destruction.

Malamud presents through fantasy and fable the tragic intensity of alienation and the desperate yearning for community in the context of total annihilation of life. Greed for arms, cold war situation and spiritual nullity in the world of today seem to lend support to Malamud's prognostication.

Though *God's Grace* differs from other Malamud's novels as it employs fantasy as technique, its essential similarity could, however, be traced to his preoccupation with compassion as a means of transformation and redemption. Malamud conveys the need of compassion through the symbolic interplay of the 'Noble Savage' and the ignoble civilized. The desperate effort of Cohn to found a community with animals, and to create a new society based on responsibility and compassionate concern for fellow being reflects Malamud's humanistic fervour and primitivistic concern. But such efforts of Cohn are bound to fail even in the Malamudian fantasy since the basic human weaknesses of lust, sexual jealousy, selfishness and the greed overtakes the Chimpanzees also, re-enacting as it were the drama of man's self-destruction. The irony is obvious—how could animals learn to be humane when men fail to be human? The only saving grace in the novel is gorilla George's offer of Kaddish to Cohn to mourn his death at the end. George merges as the 'Noble Savage.' The possibilities of good are not altogether ruled out despite the formidable fate. *God's Grace* becomes a telling commentary on the need for compassion which is the only means to save the world from the impending doom.

The novel *God's Grace* evokes "the atmosphere of the Bible, *Robinson Crusoe*, and *The Tempest*."[47] It also draws comparison with Nevil Chute's on *The Beach* which prognosticates "the deadening effect of atomic radiation in an 'electronic paradise.'"[48] In the animal world devoid of morality and compassion, Cohn cannot be successful messiah, nor has he like Prospero magical powers to set it right. The dialogues between Cohn and God reveal the irresponsibility of man more than God's inscrutable wrath. The novel in essence is not an attempt to justify the ways of God to man but to indict man's irresponsibility to man, and God comes handy as a symbolic agent to unravel this truth.

The myth of the Flood as Noah's ark recurs with a difference. The chosen few, this time only a man and a few animals, are condemned to be free but they hasten to bring their own ruin. Cohn's attempt to inspire nobility in the animals through Jewish religion fails, driving home the point that religion can be of little use in the absence of intuitive self-responsibility and fellow feeling.

Malamud's insistence on the moral priorities involved in a difficult freedom are perhaps intrinsic to the sense of 'Jewish drama' one finds in his tales—the reflection of a tradition in which distrust of nature was always strong and—more important still of 'Covenantal theology' itself tends to view "the unique ontological status of the human being as one who can transcend natural necessity and act within a context of freedom."[49] It is precisely this quest for self-transcendence that underlies the struggle of Frank Alpine or Yakov Bok. In fact, that binds all Malamud's protagonists together as sufferers for 'the way.' Consciously or unconsciously, they understand that freedom can only be achieved in the terms of moral commitment, by acts which involve surrender to others. For it is also a truism of 'covenant man' that "one may not commune with the God of the covenant if one is not responsive to the . . . needs of human beings."[50] As Cohn tells chimps, "freedom depends on mutual obligation."[51] For answer, he heard only a "petrified silence" (95).

Depicting man as a creature "subtly conceived but less well executed" (42), whose distinctive characteristic of speech is both a blessing and a danger, Malamud offers a meaningful exploration of the condition with regard to the ancient option between knowledge and belief. Anticipating mankind's imminent self-annihilation by means of 'a home-made apocalypse,' he nevertheless expresses some muted hope for a new beginning after the end. This hope is founded upon the accumulated cultural achievements which, when rightly understood, can offer values to live by, and order the chaos of contingent 'facts.' In its most basic sense, then, Malamud's intricate novel justifies the hope it upholds against heavy odds by the very fact of its existence. Making use of "the freedom to imagine the future" (175), being an imaginative projection of what might be the many precursors which it builds upon, *God's Grace* demonstrates the crucial ability of sense-making through story telling and thus testifies to the very power on which it pins its fragile hope for humankind's survival.

## II

Bernard Malamud had continually avoided questions that would attempt to make connections between his life and his fiction. However, in his nineteen pages of an autobiographical memoir, he had written: "I would write a book, or a short story, at least three times—once to understand, the second time to improve the prose, and a third time to compel it to say what it still must say."[52] He is, no doubt, a master short story writer; he explains his reaction to the art of short story writing which demands that everything must be said "quickly, fleetingly, as though two people had met for a moment in a restaurant, or a railroad station, and one had time only to tell the other they are human,"[53] and that it should have "the right weight of theme," otherwise it would become 'trivial' and ultimately it would prove to be 'didactic.' Elaborating this point, he tells Daniel Stern:

> The short story has its own pleasure. I like packing a self or two into a few pages, predicating lifetimes. The drama is terse, happens faster, aim is often outlandish. A short story is a way of indicating the complexity of life in a few pages, producing the surprise and effect of a profound knowledge in a short time. There's, among other things, a drama, a resonance of the reconciliation of opposites: much to say, a little time to say it, something like the effect of a poem.[54]

It is a coincidence that the stories in *The Magic Barrel* with their 'poetry of human relationships' should conjure 'the effect of a poem.' Though Malamud is preoccupied in these stories with the figure of the Jew, however, to see him only as the portrayer of a special case would limit the largeness of his achievement. The principal subject of *The Magic Barrel* is the ambivalence of human nature; it also deals with the themes of freedom, commitment and responsibility towards others. In a subtle manner, Malamud touches upon those aspects of the unique combination of assimilation and alienation in mid-twentieth century American culture, that it becomes difficult to find the thin line of the Jewish cultural paradox to which Kazin admits: "Since modern life is so complex that no man can possess it in its entirety, the outsider often finds himself the perfect insider."[55]

Sometimes Malamud's character's heightened inwardness follows from his or her proximity to the Old World culture. There are a number of reasons why Sobel enters "The First Seven Years" with a moral sense of "who I am and what is in my heart"[56] that Feld lacks. As a recent refugee, he embodies more of the experience of Diaspora than Feld. Feld lacks Sobel's moral intensity and the American-born Max is thoroughly assimilated into materialism that he is more moved by the job Feld does on his shoes than he is by Miriam's depths of feeling.

The story "The Mourners" is about spiritual transformation, but it is also about how a fat businessman's error drives him to wrap a sheet about himself and sink in ritual posture in a stinking tenement room. Gurber is a *Schlemiel*—a bungler who could fall on his back and break his nose. Within nine pages Malamud creates a strongly moving experience. The bleak setting of crumbling tenement serves as an appropriate backdrop for Kessler's life of self-imposed loneliness and isolation. The conditions of his apartment parallel the rotting, disordered, aimless wreckage of his life. By the end of the story, Kessler arrives at a moral insight, and what is more, causes another, Gurber, to have a shock of ironic self-recognition.

"Angel Levine" is a fantastic story. Manischevitz, a poor Jewish tailor, undergoes Job-like 'reverses and indignities.' He has lost everything, business, son, daughter; he had a wife who is hopelessly ill. He himself is too sick to work more than a few hours to maintain their bare existence. In answer to his prayer, Levine arrives, a black Jewish angel, who is "in a condition of probation" (46) until he can earn his wings through inspiring the tailor's faith. Unable to accept the idea of a Jewish angel being black, Manischevtiz rejects him, and both fall into despair. Finally, continued suffering causes tailor to acknowledge Levine as "an angel from God" Levine soars off to heaven and Manischevtiz's troubles miraculously cease. In this story Malamud uses fantasy as a unifying frame for a mixture of the comic and serious. The final line, "Believe me, there are Jews everywhere" (54), serves not only as an ironic, slightly enigmatic statement, weighted with moral meaning but as a comic device that satirizes the myth of the Jews holding the patent on suffering.

The story "Take Pity" in its enveloping despondency is reminiscent of "The Mourners." Recalling the incidence of limbo, Rosen narrates to Davidov the story of futile gestures of pity towards Eva, whose husband died of extreme indigence. Rosen tells Davidov that he was deeply moved at the plight of Axel Kalish, the Polish refugee, who ran a pisher grocery store. After Axel's death, Rosen wants Eva to take the insurance money and move out to some other place with her two girls, but Eva says that all her relatives had been murdered by the Nazis. He then suggests that she could marry someone who would look after the children, but her answer is woeful: "In my whole life I never had anything. I don't expect better. This is my life" (89). Rosen confesses that he is a man with only one kidney, and is further touched by the plight of the children: "I have a heart and I am human" (90). Determined to help her still, he wills his entire property to help her, and then in the kitchen, "I turned on the gas and put my head in the stove" (94). When the narration of events is over, Eva appears outside the room with beseeching eyes, and Rosen berates her and sends her back to the children. Perhaps, the only explanation is that after his suicide, Rosen has nothing more to give and wants that Eva should return to reclaim his testament. An exemplum of heroic altruism, the story presents a sharp contrast to the go-getting pursuits of counterfeiters.

In "The Prison," the theme of compassion is further delineated in the character of Tommy Castelli who runs a candy store with his wife, Rosa. His past is full of ignominy, and his present with Rosa in the store suffocating. The only incident which occupies his mind in the store is a young girl's act of shoplifting. He catches her more than once and is divided in his mind over the action. To his utter mortification, Rosa catches hold of the girl, and Tommy reprimands his wife for being harsh to the girl. Like Frank Alpine, Tommy is conscious of his shady past, of the dehumanizing impact of the store and wants to perform the act of human compassion, though he finds it rejected by the girl. What Malamud seems to suggest is that, despite going to good turn, one may encounter only "the mocking irony of human ingratitude."[57]

In "The Bill," Malamud emphasizes the duality of human nature in which compassion wars with self-interest, conscience with greed. A tenement janitor, Willy Schlegel, takes advantage of a neighbourly grocer, Mr. Panessa, by running up a bill of eighty-three dollars and then switching to a nearby self-service market. Obsessed by guilt, he develops a hatred for the elderly Panessa. When he receives a letter from Mrs. Panessa pleading for ten dollars for her sick husband, Willy hides in the cellar, but the next day he pawns his overcoat and runs back with money—only to discover the grocer being carried off in a coffin. Willy's sinking heart becomes "a black painted window. . . . And the bill was never paid" (136). The ending of the story makes clear to the reader that Willy has turned Mr. Panessa's gift into an emotional debt that he can never repay although it remains uncertain whether Willy himself shares the insight.

Ihab Hassan writes: "Literature has always fed on crisis but contemporary literature gives the impression sometimes of feeding on its own entrails. . . . Art is offered on the altar of reality with a dim and wild hope so that man may be reborn."[58] However, Malamud's response to the human condition is deep; it is revealed with breath-taking skill. It is the response of conscience to the incongruities of life, the quest for dignity in humiliation. The voice of conscience is audible in the beat of words, in the crackle of metaphor; it is everywhere in Malamud's work. Malamud's collection of short stories *Idiots First* takes up the alienation and self-exile in more oblique and playful fashion. The stories which have all appeared in magazines before, add to the fine testament of man's will to walk with charity and dignity.

The idea of a fancied 'new life,' the life of purpose realized through a harmonious blend between the individual and the human aspiration, is conveyed in the story "A Choice of Profession." When this harmony, for lack of compassion, fails to characterize human relations, the result is a despairing failure. Like S. Levin in *A New Life*, Cronin, after discovering that his wife "has been two timing him with a friend, suffered months of crisis," leaves Chicago to take up teaching in a small college town in Northern California. After being disappointed, he experiences a renewed enthusiasm in life when Mary Lou Miller joins his class. Once, when they are out on a drive, they tell each other about their past lives, the common experience being their having been divorced. When Cronin is getting a little more curious about her, she tells him about her life as a whore, and her having been arrested once. Cronin tries to understand her position, and wants to forgive her on the basis of being human. Besides, he thinks that, since she wants to blot out the past in her determined bid to be different, he should be liberal in his reaction to her earlier ignominy. On reflecting over her earlier fall, Cronin starts theorizing about potency of will with which the past could be totally eliminated and not allowed to meddle with the present or the future options of the individual. It is on the strength of this rationale that Cronin proposes to deepen his interest in Mary. But Mary counterpoints his enthusiasm with the revelation of her incest with her brother. The old wound opens out again with this revelation and Cronin feels that once again he is his old miserable self. Mary starts moving with his colleague, George Gets, that makes Cronin egregiously jealous of George. He tells George about Mary's past and he too grows cold towards her. Mary confronts Cronin about his role, for she had tried to confide in him. It is because of the cumulative sense of shame and failure that he leaves college and returns to Chicago. The story suggests that, despite his attempts to reorient his life, man can seldom succeed in his mission. The irony is significant: Mary, despite her past, achieves a sense of peace with herself, whereas Cronin's wound further festers. The profession that Cronin gives up, Mary hopes to adopt after she gets the degree, for teaching should mean the art of 'giving myself' to others. What Malamud seems to suggest in the reversals of Cronin is that it is easier to formulate a concept of liberal accommodation of others, but indeed, far more difficult to undergo the trial of ego-effacement.

The story "The Jewbird" is a fantasy and its central character fails his test of faith. Harry Cohen unconsciously wishes to escape his Jewishness and become a fully assimilated American. It deals allegorically with the theme of anti-Semitism. A bedraggled black jewbird named Schwartz enters through an open window of Cohen's apartment near the lower East River. Pursued by anti-Semites he seeks protection in the home of a fellow-Jew who is, however, allergic to his foul smell. In an answer to Harry's query, Schwartz says he is an old radical and prays without phylacteries. When Harry further enquires about his destination, Schwartz's caustic reply is: "Where there's charity I'll go" (104). On the insistence of his son, Maurie, the Jewbird is allowed to stay temporarily on the balcony, and he starts helping the boy with his schoolwork. When Maurie shows noticeable improvement in the school as a result of Schwartz's coaching, Harry dreams to send his son to an Ivy League college. Harry criticizes Schwartz harshly for producing the odour of dead fish. When Edie, Harry's wife asks him to take a bath to wash off his smell, Schwartz's reaction has a punch: "Everybody smells, some people smell because of their thoughts or because who they are. My bad smell comes from the food I eat" (109). Harry tries to drive him away by bringing the cat, but Schwartz cannot leave the home of a Jew because of the hazards of pogroms. Then Harry picks up courage, in the absence of Edie and Maurie, to filing him down the street. When Maurie discovers in spring a dead black bird with his neck twisted and wings broken, Maurie cries and wants to know the murderer. His mother says some 'anti-Semites' must have done it. What Malamud seems to convey through this fable is that there are Jews and Jews, and they can be as cruel as the philistines. The value of tenderness that renders life purposeful remains unappreciated by the insensitive mind of Harry Cohen. "If 'Angel Levine' suggests that Jews (metaphorically) are everywhere, 'The Jewbird' demonstrates the opposite, that anti-Semites are everywhere; even a Jew can become one by denying part of himself and losing his sense of humanity."[59]

In the "Pictures of Fidelman," its protagonist, Arthur Fidelman has gone from America to Rome to 'prepare a critical study of Giotto.' This collection consists of six episodes and in each one of them Fidelman progresses from alienation to reconciliation with art, humanity, his Jewish heritage and himself. In "Last Mohican" Fidelman is persecuted by his own Jewishness, in the form of Susskind, an exiled Israeli. Fidelman is writing a book on Giotto. Susskind steals and burns it. Denied even the release of indignation or anger, Fidelman 'understands' Susskind's gesture and in return to the charity and humility, that he now sees as his only talent, he gives Susskind one of his two suits.

In "Still Life," however, Fidelman persevers again, masochistically falling in love with an Italian girl who will have nothing to do with him until he denies his identity by paining her as Madonna and himself as a priest. "Naked Nude" finds Fidelman blackmailed—through a series of improbable events—into painting a copy of Titian's 'Venus of Urbino.' The plan is to substitute the copy and make off with the original, but at the last moment—in an absurd affirmation—Fidelman chooses to keep his own work. "A Pimp's Revenge" puts Fidelman in bed with Esmeralda, a young whore. Trying unsuccessfully to complete a painting of himself and his mother that has tortured him for years, Fidelman hits on the idea of having Esmeralda model for the mother, hoping that this will give new impetus to the project. The painting turns out to be a masterpiece, but instead of 'mother and son,' it is 'Prostitute and Procurer.'

The story "Picture of the Artist" is a heavy work of quotation maundering about art, truth and devil. And "Glass Blower of Venice" finds Fidelman sleeping now with Margherita, until her homosexual husband Beppo ambushes and rapes him in the same bed. Fidelman then learns love and 'glass blowing'—a peculiarly complex pun on Malamud's part—and takes these accomplishments back to America.

Fidelman is quintessential Malamud hero, the *Schlemel*; his name ironically refers to Fidelman's inordinate faith in his artistic ability and to the fidelity he displays in his pursuit of perception in both life and work. If his vulnerable good will suggests Morris Bober, Fidelman's experience closely parallels Frank Alpine's. From frustration in "Last Mohican" through sexual bewitchment in "Still Life," Fidelman reaches in "Naked Nude" an imprisonment. It parallels Frank's incarceration in the Bober grocery store at the end of *The Assistant*.

The sufferings of Malamud characters seem like combination of fate, and their own mistakes. Fidelman's fate, however, seems largely self-created; all his suffering appears to derive from his wrong choices and his blind selfish behaviour. Throughout *Pictures of Fidelman*, the idea of suffering and responsibility have played a subtle thematic counterpoint to Fidelman's overriding quest for success in life and in art. These themes and the character of Fidelman himself have drawn these six stories together into a loose novelistic unity they would not otherwise have. Samuel Bellman recognized the dynamic possibilities of the bumbling artist when he describes Fidelman as a character, "constantly growing, realizing himself, transforming his unsatisfactory old life into a more satisfactory new one."[60] By finally abandoning the pretences of an essentially dishonest art for honesty of simple craftsmanship, and by transcending selfishness through the acceptance of love, Fidelman manages to reconcile the claims of the head and the heart. If some degree of suffering is inescapable in every man's fate, Fidelman has learned at last that it need not be aggravated by foolish behaviour and selfish choices. He has also shown that the denial of destructive lust, for the sake of selfless and responsible love, can in the end lead 'a new and better life.'

In the epigraph to *Rembrandt's Hat* are mentioned two quotations: one from T.S. Eliot and the other from James T. Field's comment to Henry James: "What we want is short cheerful stories." These eight stories, by no means short, are neither wholly cheerful nor totally depressing but a mixed fare like most of the human situations. Eliot's line: "And an old white horse galloped away in the meadow," is sharply counterpointed with Malamud's horse in one of the stories in the collection, for this horse does not possess the swiftness and freedom of Eliot's horse nor does it gallop in the meadow, for the phenomenal urbanization has banished the meadows from American landscape. Both the quotations in the epigraph tend to suggest the irony of human situations conceived and rendered in the book. Owing to the antithesis between the import of these quotations and pervasive sadness in most of the stories, Michael is right in observing that the epigraphs "express a kind of pain in his [Malamud's] heart."[61]

All the stories deal primarily with spiritual isolation of communication that ultimately describes the alienation and self-exile of the characters. Malamud's most original accomplishment is "Talking Horse" which crowns this collection. The other stories, as it has been discussed in the preceding chapter, focus on communication failure between man and man. "Talking Horse" is a fine allegory on the struggle between man and God. It shimmers with implications on the unknowable nature of truth, and the problems of the animal yoked to the spiritual. Malamud's God is a deaf-mute horse-owner Goldberg, and man is being trapped inside the awkward body of a horse named Abramowitz. Abramowitz has been there for years, and still does not understand the nature of his fate: Goldberg-god does not talk to him very often, if at all, and seems to punish him a great deal. The worst punishment of all, however, is "when you don't know what you have to know."[62] After all, "He has his mysteries" (147). This is more than a fascinating fantasy. It is an existential statement on man's search for identity, acceptance and freedom.

In Malamud's fiction, self-transcendence is a painful process for the protagonists because it involves a great deal of suffering usually connected in some way to an elaborate and ritualistic trial of love. Malamud's protagonists appear to demand the love of people they meet. The possession of someone's love is to him an assurance of his acceptance and authenticity. The next chapter takes up this issue.

# NOTES

1. David L. Stevenson, "Fiction's Unfamiliar Face," *Nation*, 627 (November 1, 1958) 309.
2. Issac Rosenfeld, *Age of Enormity* (Cleveland: World Publishing, 1962) 69.
3. Maurice Friedman, *The World of Existentialism* (New York: Avon Books, 1964) 64.
4. *Ibid.*, 120.
5. Peter Axthelm, *The Confessional Novel* (New Haven: Meridian Books, 1967) 9.
6. *Ibid.*
7. Sigmund Freud, *Civilization and Its Discontents* (London: Random House, 1964) 120.
8. Theodore Solotaroff, *The Red Hot Vacuum and Other Pieces on the Writing of the Sixties* (New York: Atheneum, 1970) 73.
9. Robert Rogers, "The Mirror Image," *A Psychoanalytic Study of the Double in Literature* (Detroit: Wayne State Univ. Press, 1970) 29.
10. Bernard Malamud, *The Natural* (Harmondsworth: Penguin, 1967) 141.
11. C.P. Keppler, *The Literature of the Second Self* (Arizona: Univ. of Arizona Press, 1972) 194.
12. *Ibid.*, 200.
13. Sheldon J. Harshinow, *Bernard Malamud* (New York: Frederick Unger, 1980) 23.
14. *Ibid.*, 27.
15. C.P. Keppler, 202.
16. *Ibid.*
17. Bernard Malamud, *The Assistant* (Harmondsworth: Penguin, 1967) 79.
18. Alfred Kazin, "Fantasist of the Ordinary," *Commentary*, 24: 1 (July 1957) 90.
19. H.E. Francis, "Bernard Malamud's Everyman," *Midstream*, 7 (1961) 94.
20. Charles Alva Hoyt, "Bernard Malamud and the New Romanticism," *Bernard Malamud and the Critics*, ed. Leslie A. Field and Joyce W. Field (New York: New York Univ. Press, 1970) 75.
21. Bernard Malamud, *A New Life* (New York: Avon, 1980) 177.
22. Ruth B. Mandel, 110.

23. Sidney Richman. *Bernard Malamud* (New York: Twayne, 1966) 79.
24. Marcus Klein, "Bernard Malamud: The Sadness of Goodness," *After Alienation: American Novel in Mid-Century* (New York: The World Publishing, 1965) 248.
25. Marc L. Ratner, "Style and Humanity in Malamud's Fiction," *Massachusetts Review*, 5: 4 (1964) 672.
26. Mark Goldman, "Comic Vision and the Theme of Identity," *Critique*, 6: 2 (1964-65) 105.
27. Sidney Richman, 87.
28. David L. Stevenson, "The Activist," *Daedalus*, 92: 2 (Spring 1963) 249.
29. Sidney Richman, 83.
30. Tony Tanner, "Bernard Malamud and the New Life," *Critical Quarterly*, 10 (1968) 160.
31. Marc L. Ratner, 69.
32. Haskel Frankle, "Interview with Malamud," *Saturday Review* (September 1966) 39.
33. Qtd. James Mellard, "Four Versions of Pastoral," *Bernard Malamud and the Critics*, 104.
34. Bernard Malamud, *The Fixer* (Harmondsworth: Penguin, 1966) 259.
35. Bernard Malamud, *The Tenants* (Harmondsworth: Penguin, 1971) 150.
36. T.S. Eliot, "The Wasteland, II," *Selected Poems* (London: Faber and Faber, 1954) 67.
37. Daniel Stern, "The Art of Fiction" *Paris Review*, 61 (Spring 1975) 54.
38. Brita Lindberg-Seyersted, "A Reading of rnard Malamud's *The Tenants*," *Journal of American Studies*, 9: 1 (April 1975) 100.
39. Daniel Stern, 52.
40. Sheldon J. Harshinow, 118.
41. Philip Roth, *Reading Myself and Others* (New York: Farrar, Straus and Giroux, 1975) 70.
42. Pearl K. Bell, "Heller and Malamud: Then and Now" *Commentary*, 67 (June 1979) 73.
43. Mark Shechner, "The Return of the Repressed," *The Nation*, 228 (March 19, 1979) 278.
44. Bernard Malamud, *Dubin's Lives* (Harmondsworth: Penguin, 1979) 302.

45. Sheldon J. Harshinow, 143.
46. E.H.L. Masilamoni, "Bernard Malamud—An Interview," *Indian Journal of American Studies*, 9 (July 1979) 36.
47. Clive Sinclaire, "The Falling-Out in Paradise," *Times Literary Supplement* (October 29, 1982) 1188.
48. Srinivas Iyengar, "In this year of anxiety: Anno Bombini 40," *The Hindu* (July 17, 1984) 17.
49. David Hartman, *A Living Covenant: The Innovative Spirit in Traditional Judaism* (New York: Free Press, 1985) 23.
50. *Ibid.*, 31.
51. Bernard Malamud, *God's Grace* (Harmondsworth: Penguin, 1982) 12.
52. Bernard Malamud, *Long Work, Short Life: The Benningten Chapbook in Literature* (Bennington, Vt.: Bennington College, 1985) 19.
53. Qtd. *Conversations with Bernard Malamud*, ed. Lawrence Lasher (London: Univ. Press of Mississippi, 1991) 12-13.
54. *Ibid.*, 67.
55. "Under Forty: A Symposium on American Literature and the Young Generation," *Contemporary Jewish Record*, 4 (February 1944) 35.
56. Bernard Malamud, *The Magic Barrel* (Harmondsworth: Penguin, 1968) 14.
57. Ben Siegel, 208.
58. Ihab Hassan, "The Hope of Man," *New York Times Book Review*, (October 13, 1963) 5.
59. Bernard Malamud, *Idiots First* (New York: Farrar, Straus and Giroux, 1963) 80.
60. Sheldon J. Harshinow, 125.
61. Leonard Michaels, "*Rembrandt's Hat*," *New York Review of Books* (September 20, 1973) 38.
62. Bernard Malamud, *Rembrandt's Hat* (Harmondsworth: Penguin, 1976) 135.

## The Quest for Love

In a time that has emphasized the alienation and fragmentation of man, Bernard Malamud affirms the potentials of human existence. Indeed, he has extended the tradition of the romance-novel and made the form into something uniquely and significantly his own. Jonathan Baumbach writes:

> Since 1945 the serious novel has moved away from naturalism and the social scene to explore the underside of consciousness (the heart of darkness), delineating in its various ways the burden and ambivalence of personal responsibility in a world which accommodates evil—that nightmare landscape we all inhabit.[1]

In his novels, Malamud writes of the conflicting demands of the inner and outer world of his protagonist. His fiction delineates the broken dreams and private griefs of the spirit, the need of the heart, the pain of loss and the economy of love.

Malamud's characters begin as self-centred and frustrated individuals with a frightened need for success and status. Their basic drives are erotic in nature. Self-transcendence is a painful process for them because it involves a great deal of suffering usually connected in some way to an elaborate and ritualistic trial of love. This trial by love eventually forces a self-scrutiny in which protagonists realize their past mistakes and the need to be concerned for others.

Malamud's protagonists appear to demand the love of the people they meet. The possession of someone's love is to them an assurance of their identity and authenticity. It has been observed:

> Love is the redemptive grace in Malamud's fiction . . . love rejected, love misplaced, love betrayed, loveless lust; these are the main evils in Malamud's fictional world. . . . Yet the world for all

> its potential goodness, is not good, and the good man, the man capable of love, is inevitably the sufferer, the sacrificer, the saint.[2]

*The Natural* is the story of Roy Hobbs, an untrained, natural baseball player and his crucial rise and fall. The novel, Malamud reveals, is inspired by the question "Why does a talented man sell out?"[3] which suggested a moral problem. Roy's frenzied pursuits of money, fame and sex, his refusal to learn from suffering and his inability to come out of the shell of egotism—all lead to his moral disintegration. Baseball or human relations call a code of conduct and hence his failure both in human relations and baseball. However, suffering ultimately makes him realize the value of love and responsibility—"the God-given fire of decency and determination, that enables him to overcome everything arrayed against him."[4]

Roy fails to see beyond his own petty needs to the needs of others. His selfishness and egoism are easy to observe on "Roy Hobbs Day"[5] which his ebullient fans observe in honour of their hero. Exultant with success, Roy forgets that he is supposed to, "thank them for their favour and say what a good team the Knights were and how he enjoyed working for Pop Fisher" (108). In proud confidence he declares, "I will do my best—the best I am able—to be the greatest there ever was in the game" (108). The fans who elevate him to the height he reaches are of no consideration to Roy. He feels no love and no responsibility towards them. "The fans dearly loved Roy but Roy did not love the fans" (158).

Iris extols him to be a hero for others rather than best for the satisfaction of his own egoistic needs. She tells him, "I hate to see a hero fail. There are so few of them . . . without heroes we're all plain people and don't know how far we can go" (145). She wants him to give his best as a man and not just as a player to his fans.

The main focus of the novel is on Roy's personal moral failure and it shows mainly in his immature attitude towards the two women who come into his life in "Batter-up!" While Harriet represents both the evil and the good in the preface, now, the two aspects of his psyche are very distinctly portrayed in the two different persons—Memo and Iris. In Memo is epitomized Roy's selfish nature and in Iris the better side of his personality. "Character is fate," is true of Roy to the extent that Roy, in spite of his experience with Harriet, is just the incarnation of the destructive goddess Harriet Bird; like her, Memo favours black in dress. Roy is fatally attracted to the vindictive Memo who has a "sick breast"—as do all of Malamud's corrupt women, and also flaming red hair, another Malamudian sign of a diabolical nature. It is she who will tempt him to his downfall.

In his "loveless lust" for the sterile Memo, Roy neglects Iris Lemon. Iris is the fertility goddess of the mythical world. In Malamud's imagery fertility is associated with fruits and it is there in Iris Lemon's name. Another sure sign of Iris's fecundity is in her grandmother status at the age of thirty-three and her pregnancy by Roy. It is a flaw in his character which makes him lust for Memo and not respond to the wholesome love that Iris offers him. Memo would fulfil his own selfish physical needs while love of Iris would mean more giving than taking. "For Malamud's affirmation carnal love alone is not acceptable."[6] Roy must deny his carnal love for Memo for the ideal of complete love.

Roy rejects Iris because he cannot reconcile himself to the fact that Iris is a grandmother. He feels he is no "sucker" to be interested in a grandmother. He does not realize that her fertility is just what recommends Iris. He cannot imagine himself being a grandfather, though only in name: "It was simple enough to him, if he got serious with her it would lead to one thing—him being a grandfather. God save him from that for he personally felt as young and frisky as a colt" (155). However, "Attitude to the role of paternity is crucial in Malamud, and Roy refuses it."[7]

Roy knows that Iris has redemptive powers for it was she, "so cleanly etched in light" (137), who had stood up to show her confidence in him during his batting slump. She, a stranger, had expressed such faith in him as nobody else ever had, "usually when he was down he was down alone, without flowers or mourners" (141). As a consequence of her action, she loses her privacy. However, she accepts the loss with good grace for she feels, "I don't think you can do anything for anyone without giving up something of your own" (145-46), thereby magically restoring his batting potency. Roy once again sends the ball flying "through the light and up in to the dark like a white star seeking and old constellation" (139).

On the other hand, Memo "is unlucky and always has been and I think there is some kind of whammy in her that carries her luck to other people" (199). As soon as Roy goes into a slump, she begins to avoid him. Later when he is back at top of the game, she comes back to him. She confesses, "there are some things I just can't take and one of them is being with people who are blue" (156).

Roy is subconsciously aware of the worth of Iris in contrast to Memo. Yet, he does not face reality in wilful blindness. He continues to live in the illusion that Memo will build him a home and a family. Roy does realize the worth of Iris which is also evident in the fact that it is only to her he unlocks his past sufferings, his despair and dreams. It is to her he blurts out, "My god-damn life din't (sic) turn out like I wanted it to. . . . I wanted everything" (146). In Malamud's world, confession usually signifies the "dawn of love."

Having rejected Iris for her fecundity, Roy tries to divert his mind by seeking the satisfaction of his own sterile lust. Thus we see him smother his regenerative energies by indulging his own weak self. He seeks to pacify his own guilty conscience by eating. He "gluts the hunger for rebirth and the pangs of unwilling love by eating."[8] Not only is his self-preoccupation sterile, it is also self-destructive. As Harriet Bird had done earlier, this time Memo Paris leads Roy to a symbolic death by tempting him to over-eat; it gives him severe stomachache near the crucial day of the pirates-knights match.

Having rejected Iris who was wholly relaxing and satisfying, Roy longs for Memo though he realizes, "there was something about her, like all the food he had lately been eating that left him, after having of it, unsatisfied, sometimes even with a greater hunger than before" (156). Memo, like Daisy Fay, is a false goddess; she confesses, "I'm afraid to be poor" (181). The two are characteristic of American materialism at its worst. It is Memo who first suggests Roy accept the big bribe Judge Banner has to offer if he agrees to throw the play-off game. When the Judge himself first comes to the hospital to bribe Roy, he sticks to honesty for he feels he cannot betray his own team and manager. As soon as the Judge hints that he may lose Memo to Gus Sand, Roy becomes vulnerable to corruption. By this selfish act, Roy shows a great moral lapse towards others. He fails in his responsibility towards his spiritual father "Pop" who is a morally integrated man. Pop had rejected outrightly to co-operate with Judge Goodwill Banner and Gus Sand in any shady deal however beneficial to him.

Roy is not an evil person, he is just infantile. Like Malamud's heroes, Roy is the image of the unintegrated man, the hero who acts incorrectly despite his awareness."[9] Roy is half-aware of his growing corruption, yet being a weak character he continues to indulge in his weaknesses. During the final game for the pennant against the Pirates we see the better self of Roy in a tussle with his corrupt self. Having decided to throw-off the game he struggles to keep himself from batting well to win for the sake of his team and Pop Fisher.

The process of becoming a moral man is the process of learning to love. After his downfall in the end, Roy's renewed possibilities for life can come only through a commitment to love and he does seem to realize that "Evil is the denial of love and furthermore the lack of reciprocity."[10] Roy can redeem himself by reciprocating the love Iris has to offer to him. Thus Roy is given a second chance to make something of his life and redeem his loveless state by loving Iris and taking on the responsibility of her family.

Malamud has remarked that the "devaluation [of man] exists because he accepts it without protest."[11] Through the ordeal of consciousness, Roy tends to assert his dignity and freedom and differentiate between lust and love, between self-glorification and self-education. In the beginning, "talk about his inner self" was to Roy "like ploughing up a graveyard" (155). In the end, he articulates his response by confessing that he has to "suffer again." He has come to realize through his deception and failure that in his 'second' life, the experience of suffering would teach him 'to want right things.' Being a drama of the growth of inwardness, Malamud's first novel is related to the spectrum of his successive creative endeavour.

In *The Assistant*, Malamud indicates that Frank Alpine's rebirth through suffering is continued and invigorated by love which seems finally the only means of breaking through the barriers of self. In Frank's situation, the process of his redemption and of learning to love are identical. But the hero's love must transcend the central level if he has to succeed in his struggle for recognition and identity.

Frank Alpine's attraction to Helen Bober plays a significant role in achievement of authenticity and acceptance. This suggests that Malamud is close to the Hasidic teaching—that is, in the humanizing power of love. In his search for love, Frank is drawn to Helen by her capacity for suffering. They share a common desire to undo the past, and, if possible, to start all over again. They are drawn to each other mainly through the denial of their individuality by Ida Bober who is overanxious to prevent a meeting of her marriageable daughter and their Gentile assistant. Her ill-concealed anxiety and the implicit denial of Helen's identity are mainly responsible for increasing interest Helen takes in Frank. Helen is, like Frank, seeking recognition as an individual through her search for love.

The quest for love plays a significant part in Frank's success with regard to the other aspects of his quest for identity. This is his desire to evolve an enduring relationship with Morris Bober. These two strands follow a common pattern of error, repentance and repetition of the error. Frank's desire to be esteemed and loved by Helen ultimately finds his salvation in his willingness, "to suffer and sacrifice everything selfish for that love."[12] At this stage, however, Frank is dominated by his ego and he is seen here in the aspect of lover as luster, in contrast to the 'lover as provider' which he ultimately becomes.

Frank's attraction to Helen is an uneasy fusion of the sensual and the spiritual: at one moment he lusts for her; at another, he is filled with profound tenderness for her suffering. Yet, even after he comes to know her, she remains unreal to him, a personification of beauty in the world from which the conditions of existence have shut him off. Since he believes that his beauty is justifiably inaccessible to him, he compulsively destroys the relationship at the very moment when its realization becomes possible. While they are still strangers, Frank's unrequited desire for Helen impels him to climb an elevator shaft to spy on her in the bathroom to make love to her inaccessible nakedness with his desperate eyes. In a stunningly powerful scene, Malamud describes the self-induced torment of Frank's shame. Frank peeps through the bathroom window not so much to gratify his lust as to torture himself. This scene, in which Frank symbolically violates Helen, anticipates his actual violation of her later on.

Nat Pearl, Louis Karp, Ward Minogue and Frank Alpine court Helen's love in one way or another. Helen is both practical and idealistic, less ordinary than her surroundings though not extraordinary enough to surmount them. Her dream of bettering herself is an admixture of voyeurism and genuine sensibility. What she wants, as she puts it, is "the return of possibilities,"[13] though she is only vaguely aware of what her possibilities include. The unambitious liquor clerk, Louis Karp, is not good enough for her, but she is more than willing to settle for the equally shallow Nat Pearl, an ambitious law student who has apparently risen above his surroundings. It is a part of her tragedy that the real Nat is not the dream hero she has romantically envisioned. Insensitive to her, he devalues the gift of her love, taking it as his due, and irreparably wounds the giver. That Helen's dream hero of a better life might be satisfied by marriage to Nat suggests the inadequacy of her aspirations. Whereas she loses the possibility of a real relationship with Frank by withholding herself too long. When Helen is finally sure that she loves Frank, it has become too late.

Melodramatic circumstances (fate as authorial prerogative) conspire against the ill-fated lovers. While Helen is willing for

Frank in the park to tell him that she loves him, Ward Minogue also appears in his place and attempts to molest her. When after saving her from Ward Minogue, Frank forcibly makes love to her, she feels disgraced, as if Ward had actually consummated his attempt. In the merging of the acts, the two identities seem as one. Though circumstances contrive against them, Helen and Frank are in themselves responsible (fate as character) for the failure of their relationship. A Malamudian irony: Helen is able to love Frank only until he makes love to her; the fact debauches the illusion.

Having lost Helen through his lust, Frank, waking from a guilt-ridden nightmare, has a revelation about himself:

> [He] got up to run but he had run everywhere. There was no place left to escape to. The room shrank. The bed was flying up to him. He felt trapped—sick, wanted to cry but couldn't. He planned to kill himself, at the same minute had a terrifying insight: that all the while he was acting like he wasn't, he was really a man of stern morality. (157)

Like S. Levin, Frank discovers, during the period of this introspection, that he is a man of principle, but unlike Levin he is at the same time a compulsive sinner. His own most merciless judge, Frank, continually sets up occasions in which he can test his actual self against his ideal of himself. Guilty of imperfection, the presumption of the romantic hero, he debases himself as personal as penance; he destroys his relationship with Helen and continues to steal gratuitously from the grocery store. Since he wants more than anything else to be a good man, his crimes are a means of self-punishment; each time he pockets money from Morris's register, he torments himself with guilt. Moreover, he increases his debt psychologically and financially to the grocer, which means he must punish himself still further to make requital. As a penitent, he must fall deeper and deeper into his interior here before he can allow himself salvation.

At Morris's burial, when Helen tosses into the grave, Frank falls in after it, landing feet first on the coffin. It is an absurd incident, embarrassing the solemnity of the occasion; yet it is also a kind of spiritual communion between Morris and Frank. In entering the grave, Frank achieves final identification with Morris, which is the ultimate act of self-sacrifice. His rising from the grave as Morris is a symbolic resurrection. Ironically, Frank's rebirth leads him to the assumption of Morris's living death in the tomb of the grocery store. In a haunting bitter passage, Ida and Helen console each other:

> "Your father is better off dead," said Ida. As they toiled up the stairs they heard the dull cling of the register in the store and knew the grocer was the one who had danced on the grocer's coffin. (206)

Like Morris, Frank becomes wholly committed to the store, sacrificing his energies to support Ida and Helen. Taking the store as his 'bride' and accepting the worries it entails and in sharing the sorrow of the Jews who visit it, Frank has "relinquished childhood and become a new man."[14] It is the least Frank can do for the man he has wronged. In suffering for Morris's role, for all of us, Frank achieves his redemption becoming at last a wholly honest and good man. Where Helen had formerly esteemed Frank for his "possibilities," she now respects him for what he is, instead of what he might be, in terms of degrees and diplomas. Frank's redemption is made possible by his uncompromising love for Helen which provides the impetus for his commitment to the store. The amount of love a man is able and willing to commit to life is, in Malamud's universe, the measure of his grace.

Malamud's third novel *A New Life* is concerned basically with modern man's quest for identity and acceptance on social and emotional levels. S. Levin's search for emotional identity in the form of love manifests itself first as a search for human companionship. But his colleagues in the Cascadia College are all emotionally crippled, and each is the prisoner of some ruling passion which isolated him from others. Levin's isolation and his need for love involves him in a slightly comic incident with a waitress, Laverne. With the ill-luck characteristic of a *Schlemiel*, he is robbed not only of sexual fulfilment but of his cloths as well by his rival, a Syrian student, Sadak. Levin's ineffectiveness in love is due to the conflict between his deep-seated morality and the compulsion of his physical body.

Levin's conscious resolve to avoid emotional, especially sexually entanglements, cannot be sustained for long because of his compelling need for companionship. His attempt to resist the "compulsion of sexuality"[15] proves futile; he is drawn to his spinster colleague, Avis Filss, with whom he makes an abortive attempt at intercourse. Levin's innate integrity is seen in his respect for her individuality and in his not wishing to use her as an object of his lust. On seeing her damaged breast, he gives up the attempted intercourse, telling, "Poor Dame—she has little why should I make it less?" (113)

S. Levin's relationship with Pauline Gilley is a fresh start in his quest for love. He initially conceives of love as something optional, coming only after sex and makes the mistake of thinking of identity in isolation, in an emotional vacuum. This immaturity of his attitude is reflected in his exhilaration after his meeting with Pauline in the woods. But this exhilaration is tempered by the warning from the "figure within . . . against risking his new identity" (28). He counters this doubt by thinking of the incident as only 'experience' and not necessarily commitment. Levin's spiritual development is faltering, for he knows that his redemption lies in love but finds himself incapable of commitment.

Levin's dilemma is fundamentally one of separating sex from love on the level of morality. He regards Pauline Gilley not as a distinct individual but as the instrument for the attainment of love which, in turn, is his assurance of possessing identity. Pauline too is troubled by the awareness of her regarding Levin as a means of rousing her husband Gerald Gilley's jealousy and forcing recognition of her identity. Levin's agonizing review of the morality of his conduct and its retreat to his career reminds us of Frank Alpine's tortured self-examination following his rupture with Morris and Helen Bober.

Levin's earlier determination to renounce Pauline and his plans for a teaching career are upset by her decision to break away from her husband and rejoin Levin. She tries to be a "better mother and wife" (285). Having failed, she is dissatisfied with living half a life. The situation places Levin in a trying position as he has to choose love and commitment. This is a crucial stage in Levin's quest, for love is the 'redemptive grace' in Malamud's novels; it is the highest good. As such, his rejection of love would mean that he has failed in his quest. Though the choice is certainly important, Levin cannot decide at the moment but after much suffering chooses love and commitment.

Levin's prevarication over accepting Pauline's love is forcibly ended when she expresses her wish to make their relationship known to her husband. Levin realizes that he feels no love for her though he "beat himself into a concrete frenzy to resuscitate his love for her" (289). He is alarmed by her plans for him in the event of his dismissal and feels his identity challenged by what he supposes to be her attempts to manipulate him. Like Roy Hobbs in *The Natural*, Levin is faced with the problem of attaining his ago as to accommodate the claims of love. At this point, Levin is still ambivalent in his attitude to Pauline feeling guilty for his inability to love her, simultaneously resenting her attempt to force a decision on him. It is after the failure of all these attempted evasions that Levin has an important insight which indicates the emergence of his identity. He realizes the fact that although "he, S. Levin, did not presently desire her in no way, diminished her as one worthy of love" (292). By a maundering course of insights and attempted evasions of their implications, Levin moves towards the final decision that if Pauline continues to love him he, "with no known cause not to, will love her" (292). From his initial position as an introspective, sensual love, Levin has become a man capable of loving on principle, of accepting responsibility for Pauline, although with some reluctance, even at the cost of the 'new life' he has come in search of. His vacillation makes him the typical anti-hero and yet, "his integrity is undeniable."[16]

When the affair with Pauline continues, Levin the "man of principle,"[17] becomes aware of ambivalence of his ideal in achieving love, he is betraying Gilley, a man who befriended him when he needed a friend. Levin's melodramatic dilemma is clearly defined: what takes priority in a world of isolation, loss, and pain—love or principle? Malamud resolves this conflict by diminishing Gilley out of existence, by making his mortality despicable that Levin's betrayal of his seems no more than just retribution. That Levin wants desperately to succeed in his new career presents a further complication. He knows that if his relationship with Pauline is discovered, he will be summarily fired. To make matters even more difficult for himself, as a 'man of principle,' he has quixotically committed himself to fight for certain needed reforms in the College. Baumbach says, "Malamud's universe is perversely whimsical; it grants boons but tarnishes them in the process; no gain is without loss."[18]

Love is sacred in the universe; if life is holy, love is also holy. At the end of the novel. Levin achieves a kind of unsought heroism in sacrificing his career for the principle of love, a love in itself dead, a memory beyond feeling. Accepting responsibility for having once been in love with Pauline, Levin agrees to marry her, to take on the burden of her two sickly children which gives up hope of teaching in the college again. The knowledge of Duffy's death further influences Levin's decision. In leaving Cascadia with Pauline and her two adopted children, he is fulfilling an implicit commitment to Duffy, who has been the example of his behaviour. Thus, Levin's act of heroism becomes, in another context, an act of love.

The quality of this heroism is defined in his last confrontation with Gilley. When, as a favour to Pauline, Levin asks her rejected husband for custody of the children, Gilley responds by pointing out to his successor the prohibitive drawbacks of marrying a chronically discontented woman and assuming responsibility for a ready-made family. When Levin, against all logic, seems bent on going through with his decision, Gilley is amazed: "An old woman than yourself and not dependable, plus two adopted kids, no choice of yours no job or promise of one, and other assorted headaches. Why take that load on yourself?" (304). But Levin retorted, "Because I can, you son of a bitch" (304). Gilley's plea to him to leave them alone and go to another college precipitates Levin's determination to take her away from the dull and self-satisfied Cascadia campus. That he is not deterred from his course by Gilley's promise of good references or by his recital of Pauline's drawbacks and of the children's ailments, underlies Levin's emergence with identity as a moral man although Levin resents being formed into the role of Pauline's "saviour or victim" (312).

This problem is solved for him when he learns that she is pregnant with his child. The attainment of fatherhood is the mark of maturity and this vital change is reflected in his rejection of Pauline's offer to have an abortion, as also in the declaration, "I want the child" (314). His love for Pauline is now transformed into "a new and non-romantic form."[19] What Levin has done is not the repudiation of his old self but has accommodated his ego to the claims of love. Though Levin is not better off in material terms, he has definitely grown up and has developed a mature attitude to love. Ultimately, Levin attains self-knowledge and recognition through love.

*A New Life* is principally about Levin's heroic destiny: his discovery of what it is and his acceptance of what it entails. The other characters, with the possible exception of Pauline are caricatures and stereotypes, part of the allegorical landscape of Levin's quest. Malamud is at his best in this curiously flawed novel in illuminating Levin himself—the underside of his consciousness, the arena of his dark, hallucinated dreams, his war with the past and his uneasy peace with the future.

As in the case of Frank Alpine and S. Levin, romantic love is one of the constituents of Yakov Bok's quest for recognition and identity in Malamud's novel *The Fixer*, though this aspect of his quest is initially obscured by his preoccupation with women. His upbringing and experience had taught Yakov to regard love as luxury and an incapacity to love is a feature that he shares with Levin. Like Levin, he makes the mistake of separating sex from love, and it is this "psychic flaw"[20] in him that was responsible for his wife's childlessness. His rather comic encounter with Nikolei's daughter Zina highlights this deficiency in him. He is unable to make love to Zina because she is "unclean" and, he confesses that love "does not come easily to him."[21] His response to Zina "glosses vividly his wretched marriage with Raisl" and reveals his obsessive concern "with his own security" (3).

Yakov leaves the *Shtetl* to find meaning in life. He wants to get rid of his unhappy childhood and the wasted past. But in anti-Semitic Kiev, he is allegedly charged with the 'ritual' murder of a Christian boy. He is an isolated individual and seeks for "accommodation" in the new environment. His prolonged imprisonment helps him see the worth of life through the means of suffering. It is through suffering and love for others that he attains his identity and authenticity.

His wife Raisl comes to meet him in the prison. His resentment against her is increased when he learns that she had a child by the Jewish musician with whom she had eloped. But Yakov's encounter with Raisl has a positive aspect in that it makes him realize that the responsibility for the failure of marriage is at least partly his own. Here, Yakov faces the crucial test of his maturity that he has after his imprisonment.

Yakov's movement from alienation to "accommodation"[22] is marked by his growing tolerance of his wife Raisl and his understanding of the factors behind his desertion. His reminiscences of courting Raisl and of his life with her lead him to adopt a more comprehensive and sympathetic attitude to her infidelity to him: "But now, I look at it, like this: she had tied herself to the wrong kind of future" (299). Yakov's developing response to his past and his experience make him more cognizant to his failure and his responsibility for it, and more capable of compassion. This attainment of spiritual maturity is reflected in his willingness to declare himself the father of the bastard child. This symbolic assumption of paternity redeems his former failure and with this heroic acceptance of commitment he has come to "What is at the heart of the Judeo-Christian moral idea. His horrid life now has meaning and puprpose."[23] It shows him capable of charity and compassion which he had lacked as a "free man." His sense of responsibility for Raisl and his love for her leads him to attain his identity and authenticity.

After the novel *The Tenants* appeared, Steven G. Killmen complained that Malamud had made only a passing reference to the Korean War and Vietman war, "an involvement which threatened as much destruction to American society as it entailed on the Asian mankind."[24] However, Malamud's focus is on the impact of the tense times on the humanity symbolically represented in the mutual hatred, suspicion and guilt of the black and the Jewish writers, Harry Lesser and Willie Spearmint in *The Tenants*. He is worried about the lack of compassion and love in a world of growing nihilistic tendencies. Here, Malamud apparently insists upon the value of brotherhood, as the title of the novel indicates itself, and community despite the denigration of human life in modern society.

Malamud's faith in the power of love is still intact in *The Tenants*. However, the technique used is the stress on the lack of love in the world, the resultant apathy of man towards man and, therefore, the need for love. To selflessly love another is to achieve great heights in Malamud's fiction. Harry Lesser, the protagonist of *The Tenants*, is seeking love through writing. Lesser's novel is about a novelist (Lazer) writing a novel about a novelist; it deals with a similar problem—the writer's incapacity to love and show compassion. Malamud tells us, "this writer [Lesser] sets out to write a novel about someone he conceives to be not he yet himself. He thinks he can teach himself to love in a manner befitting an ideal . . . he invents this character in his book who will in a sense love for him . . . which is perhaps to say . . . that Lesser's writer in his book is creating love as best he can, if he can bring it off in imagination will extend self and spirit."[25]

Lesser's novel is ironically titled *The Promised End*; the end is as elusive as the epigraph to *The Tenants* from *King Lear*: "who is it that can tell me who I am?"[26] Lesser is convinced that if he can work out an ending, he will discover what love is. His chances of doing so, however, are not promising. He can find no ending of ideal love to his book, because it parallels his own life of unfulfilment. Even when he gets a chance to love in real life, Lesser does not take it. In *The Tenants*, Irene Bell represents love and the hope of redemption in life. Rebirth is possible when

Irene and Lesser were serious about making a future together. Then it was spring—the time of rejuvenation. For a short time Lesser experiments with the complexities of love but basically he is unwilling to surrender to anything which come in the way of his writing, "he would never abandon this novel, never, for whatever reason; nor would anything good or bad, Levenspiel, Bill Spear, for instance, or any woman, black or white, persuade him to give it up" (88).

Though Lesser has, for the time, moved away from his rigid discipline, consciously yet he remains occupied with his book. "There's no half way to a writer," he tells Irene, even he understands that "because of Irene he lived now with a feeling of more variously possessible possibilities, an optimism that boiled up imagination. Love's doing" (116). Unfortunately, this 'love's doing' must wait till he has finished his novel. Malamud declares, "The struggle of his characters against self is 'basic.' Certainly his heroes resist the truths conveyed by their reflections and fears. Mostly losers, they opt invariably for defeat or failure, even with success or happiness in view. They can thank ill-luck, moral flaw or sheer stupidity."[27] Lesser is as much a *Schlemiel* as Malamud's other heroes.

Unable to love in life, Lesser is unable to achieve a perfect ending to his novel of ideal love. He tried out three dream endings—all products of his overwrought imagination. The ending is Lesser's fantasy of 'double wedding' of himself and Mary and Willie and Irene. "Here's this double wedding going on, that's settled in his mind" (156), dreams Lesser. The ritual of the unconventional marriages between blacks and whites performed by the risk-taking priest is graphically portrayed. Even in dream, Lesser confesses to Mary his inability to love. He says, "Mary, I am short of love in my nature, don't ask me why, but I'll try to give you your due" (161). The rabbi preaches the value of love and mutual trust to the black and white couple:

> Willie and Irene, to enjoy the pleasures of the body you don't need a college education; but to live together in love is not so easy. Besides love that which preserves marriage is that which preserves life; this is mutual thrust, insight into each other, generosity, and

> also character, so that you will do what is not easy to when you must do it. What else can I tell you, my children? Either you understand or you don't. (163)

The rabbi also longs for amity between the blacks and the whites. "Someday God will bring together Ishmael and Israel to live as one people. It won't be the first 'miracle'" (164) and the hope of the rabbi is very much the hope of Bernard Malamud.

Malamud's novel *Dubin's Lives* delves into the psyche of a middle-aged man, William B. Dubin, wrecked with the problem of sex, love and infidelity. Having experimented with a novelist in *The Tenants*, Malamud here provides a creative insight into the craft of biography. Richard Gilman points out, the 'double-edged' title of the novel refers at an immediate level to the lives of Thoreau, Lincoln, and Mark Twain whose lives Dubin writes, and, "more poetically to the divisions within his own being."[28] Robert Rubenstein remarks: "*Dubin's Lives* opens out to address the limits of love and marriage, of familiarity, of self-fulfilment and fiction themselves by articulating the inconsistencies and emotional contradictions of real people."[29] Malamud chooses to convey that life, with all its challenges and crises, continues to mature one's sense of priorities. Benson identifies this element in the struggle of Malamud's characters: "Perhaps Malamud's work is part of the pendulum that swings from meaning to non-meaning, back to meaning again, an answer to the nihilism of the late Fifties and Sixties, similar to T.S. Eliot's answer to the nihilism and materialism of the late Teens and Twenties."[30] Malamud seems to suggest that although it is difficult to be a champion, to realise one's trans-ethnic humanity, to crusade for democracy and liberalism, or to combat political injustice and cultural prejudice, it is tougher to make sense of one's life.

Seemingly different in form from Malamud's other novels, *Dubin's Lives* reveals the familiar stance of the writer. For Peter S. Prescott, the novel deals with the common question of Malamud: "how shall a man create for himself a new life?"[31] and the answer also remains the same, "One is reborn to life, and to one's life's work, by discovering passion, and by learning how to balance the conflicting demands of passion and commitment."[32]

The commitment and love ultimately get an upper hand over passion in Malamud's works as in *Dubin's Lives*. Yet one perceives a change in the overall tone of the novel. From the "sad-eyed ironist of human suffering," Malamud turns into "an unselfconscious celebrant of the self."[33]

Dubin is a peculiar writer who lives the lives of others and tries to understand his own self. He loves nature like Thoreau, but Lawrentian motives of sex, love and guilt haunt him. His marriage with Kitty, a widow, is a bond of convenience dictated by mutual need. Both Dubin and Kitty live in their own world away from the present—Dubin in his lives of the dead and Kitty in her reminiscences of her former husband and estranged children. Dubin at the age of fifty-six is attracted by Fanny Bick, a promiscuous girl less than half his age. He is in conflict between his obligation to his wife and passion for Fanny. His work halts and moves only when he continues his illicit contact with Fanny. He is, however, torn by a sense of guilt towards his wife. Dubin and Kitty drift from each other as Kitty has an affair with Evan Ondyk. Dubin's affair with Fanny ceases when in the end he goes back to his wife with love. The obligation to wife triumphs over the passion for mistress. The quest for love is suggested in *Dubin's Lives* in realization of one's obligations and responsibilities. However, the sense of love is considerably marred by the long descriptions of sexual bouts of Dubin with Fanny and the mechanically contrived situation of lust.

It may seem paradoxical that Dubin, a man of meagre appetites should choose Lawrence, the prophet of sexuality as the subject for his biography. The only explanation that Dubin has is that rather than choosing Lawrence, he himself, in a way, has been chosen by the writer as if he wanted Dubin to learn from his experiences. The choice, however, bears out a subconscious logic. Lawrence becomes Dubin's other self—the repressed self that craves for freedom of his hidden desires.

Malamud maintained that he chose D.H. Lawrence as Dubin's subject "because Lawrence's theories about the significant relationship of sexual experience to the deeper sources of life . . . gave Dubin things he could think about more than mere experience itself . . . so Lawrence's theories give the world of sex a kind of deepening."[34] Lawrence influences Dubin's thought process and thereby his experiences. On the other hand, his affair with Fanny "sparked his work. Ideas swarmed in Dubin's mind."[35] His own passionate experiences enhance his understanding of what Lawrence meant by "the slow invasion in you of the vast invisible God that lives in the ether—'the Old Pagan vision.'" (233). Through Fanny, he feels a "gifted man, an excellent biographer" (224). He now explicates D.H. Lawrence on sex as "Sex to him, you understand, despite his ideology of blood-being, was a metaphor for a flowering life" (224).

Lawrence's views on sex, love and women influence Dubin to the extent that there are times when Dubin becomes Lawrence the lover. Lawrence gives him the impetus to give vent to his desires and after having experienced Lawrence-like experiences in actuality, he understands the writer's views on sex, "as a dark force of blood-consciousness through which man experiences, wants man to risk himself for a platitude of life through love" (322).

As Dubin tries to comprehend the Lawrentian feeling within himself, he states, quotes and learns from Lawrence and in the process we gain insight into Dubin. "How curious it is, Dubin thought, as you write a man's life, how often his experiences become yours to live. This goes on from book to book: their lives evoke mine or why do I write? I write to know the next room of my fate. To know it I must complete Lawrence's life" (317). Lawrence exerts much influence on Dubin in spite of the fact that Dubin is aware of the contradictions in the writer's life. He knows, as we know, the ironic fact that Lawrence was impotent at a relatively young age of forty-two and his sexual manifestos were in fact a protest against his ineffectual self rather than an affirmation of his sexual liberation. "Dubin tries to be a Lawrentian hero in a Malamud world, that is, a phallic narcissist in a life of modest designs and severe consequences."[36] Naturally Lawrentian sexuality and narcissism have no place in Malamud's world of dire consequences for unexpressed desires.

Thus Malamud makes his point when he shows that liberation only brings loneliness and failure for Dubin. Fanny temporarily liberates Dubin but he does not achieve affirmation. Malamud, however, "pursues his favourite myth of moral exigency with resort to folklore or the easy affirmations of packaged morality."[37] With patience and credibility Malamud works out Dubin's fling into eroticism, the pangs of conscious and ultimately, a sane decision to return to his wife and home. Dubin's demonstration of love towards his wife is a moral act. "The moral act, no matter what moral act it is, is itself charged with significance because any moral act is difficult and unlikely."[38] Moreover, once again Malamud affirms the possibility of human change and renewal. As do all of Malamud's lonely protagonists, Dubin learns that the new life he seeks is best gained by responding to another's needs. At last, then, Dubin acts responsibly. Like S. Levin, despite his failings, Dubin has realized that life is holy rather than happy. Dubin learns that a new life full of love hinges on renewed responsibilities and not on the false conception of freedom.

The novel *God's Grace* is not a traditional apocalyptic novel but a post-apocalyptic tale which examines what might come after the cataclysm, a story that begins with the very end and tries to sound out the possibilities of a new beginning. Malamud emphasizes that the cause of destruction was man's 'self-betrayal' and God's wrath. "The war was man's: the Flood God's."[39] God roars at Cohn through the bulbous cloud: "Man after failing to use to a sufficient purpose his possibilities, and my goodwill, has destroyed himself" (12). He complains of destruction by men of everything natural and good:

> They tore apart my ozone, carbonized my oxygen, acidified my refreshing rain. Now they affront my cosmos. How much the Lord endure? . . . In sum, the evil overwhelmed the good. The Second Flood, this that now subsides on the broken earth, they brought on themselves. (13)

Malamud indicts modern civilization for destroying primitive values. The entire effort of Calvin Cohn, the lone survivor, is to realize man's errors and not to repeat them. The writer intends to stress the dreadful isolation of man through Cohn to underline the value of companionship. Cohn realizes that "right words" and "right life" acquire meaning only in relation to other human beings:

> On good days Cohn told himself stories, saying the Lord would let him live if he spoke the right words. Or lived the right life. But how was that possible without another human life around? (17)

He, however, makes a significant decision to 'live on' despite the wrathful God. On the Island, "another version of Malamudian prison,"[40] Cohn has to face the existential crisis like the primeval man assuming 'a future for better or worse.' He consoles himself that his life in the cave is "better than death." All alone, he offers Kaddish is not a mere rite but a symbol of reverence for life. He feels, "The Dead must be acknowledged if one respects life." (41). Death and destruction have brought him the value of life.

The gorilla George is a symbol of Jewish endurance and compassion in contrast to the noisy Buz. Cohn realizes that it was this gorilla that nursed him when he had fallen ill on the island because of radiation poisoning. George is the only animal to profit by Cohn's teaching both at home and at the school tree. He is moved to hear the story of Egyptian persecution of Israelites. Buz, on the contrary, appears as an antithesis, to George. Endowed with speech abilities, Buz becomes the product of modern civilization. It represents as its name indicates the noise and haste as well as the querrulousness, and finally ingratitude of modern man in its betrayal of Cohn. It always offends George and remains deaf to Cohn's lesson of compassion and love. "If we expect to go on living we have to be kind to each other" (78).

For Cohn as for a hard primitivist, animals become exemplars. He responds favourably to Mary's (the female chimpanzee) unnatural passion for him although he refuses to mate with her in the beginning. He did not agree with Buz that he is a different kind from them and says that there is only one kind on the Island, "sentient, intelligent, living beings" (164). Cohn's consummation with Mary makes his complete identification with the animals like a primitivist. It also results in the birth of a new species of "humanoid infant, or chimpanzee—human baby" (162). Cohn hopes that "she may someday be the mother of a newer race of man" (165).

The optimism kindled in Cohn for a new civilization is soon shattered by the ghastly deeds of Easu and other chimpanzees. Sex and cannibalistic violence become once again the bone of contention. Easu rapes Sara. One of the baboons newly landed on the Island. The other chimpanzees—Esterhazy, Bromberg, Saul and Luke—just remain passive spectators. Easu kills the female baboon later and eats it cannibalistically with others. Though Easu and his followers now and Buz later appear to be ignoble savages, they are in fact portrayed to represent the ignoble civilized who perished in violence. Cohn is pitted against them with his missionary zeal to humanize the brutes. His admonition, "If you depreciate lives, the worth of your own diminishes" (174). Easu attacks Cohn when he was exiled by the latter, and continues to kill the baboons. Cohn is now disillusioned; he felt himself a failure:

> I have failed to teach these chimpanzees a basic truth. How can they survive if they do to fellow survivors what men did to each other before the Second Flood? How will they evolve into something better than man? (183)

The apocalypse recurs. Cohn fails to protect his only hope, Rebekah (his daughter)—'the future of another civilization.' The apes kill it cruelly. Cohn accuses Buz of ingratitude for betraying the family to the murderous apes. He pulls away the knotted wires which gave Buz speech. Ironically, Buz's last words are, "I am not Buz, my name is Gottlob" (194). Things are now completely out of control. The apes at the school tree just mock at Cohn's cave and drag him up the mountain with a bundle of split wood against his chest to burn him. Cohn becomes a Christ-figure to be martyred. The son like Buz thrusts the knife into his throat. Cohn has the epiphanic awareness of god's mercy: "Merciful God," he said, "I am an old man. The Lord has let me live life out" (201). All the while Cohn had feared God more than he loved Him. He had in fact warned the chimpanzees in one of his seven admonitions that "God is not love, God is God" (157).

The prophet has failed to reform the chimpanzees and ended up as a martyr. But George, the gorilla, wearing a mudstained white yarmulke reads a long Kaddish for Cohn. It is perhaps for all the ceaseless efforts of Cohn for meaningful existence. As a Malamud hero, Cohn's only hope could be "to save a single soul before dying."[41] The conversion of George, however, comes off to fulfil Cohn's task partially despite the latter's failure with the chimpanzees.

Malamud does not exert "the same imaginative powers upon the macrocosm as he does upon the microcosm"[42] in the novel. It should be remembered that Malamud is not interested so much in the act of atomic destruction of human race as in the portrayal of its horrendous consequences.

## II

In the novels, Malamud's protagonists transcend the disorder that surrounds them finding meaning in the power of love and moral commitment. Malamud has written forty short stories, and most of them have been published in four volumes: *The Magic Barrel*, *Idiots First*, *Pictures of Fidelman: An Exhibition*, *Rembrandt's Hat*. Like his novels, these stories deal with moral issues and words like conscience, responsibility, love, suffering and compassion have implicit value. He recognizes that man is a compound of good and bad, and yet has the potentiality to change for better. "For Malamud the essential human failure is lovelessness, failure to recognize the humanity of others, failure to treat human beings humanely. Human and humane are overlapping categories for Malamud and the human aspiration to become humane and more human, is his central drama."[43] His interest in his fiction is in man, "in the process of changing his fate, his life."[44]

*The Magic Barrel* reveals Malamud's love of Jews, of "humanity, compassion, and all the virtues."[45] R.C. Blackman points out that "a tone of resigned and humorous wisdom and an unsentimental central compassion"[46] and love unify the stories of

*The Magic Barrel.* The tragic suffering of Panessa in "The Bill" and Lieb in "The Lone" acquire meaning in their affectionate response to the needs of the suffering brethren. Love and compassion at the cost of self-effasive suffering is poignantly evoked in the stories. The predicament of Panessa recalls that of Morris in *The Assistant.* Although poor himself, Panessa in 'The Bill' readily gives credit to Willy Schlegel. His compassion is prompted by an unflinching faith in humanity. His concept of 'credit' is the recognition of the fact "that people were human beings, and if you were really a human being you gave credit to somebody else and he gave credit to you."[47]

"The Lone" is a story of miserable people haunted by bad luck. Kobotsky could not cover the grave of his wife with a stone even after five years of her death. He approaches his old friend Lieb for a loan forgiving Kobotsky's earlier evasion of debt, but his wife objects. She is moved by the story of Kobotsky, but instead of giving the loan recounts her own tragic past which overcomes the woe of Kobotsky. As the loaves in the tray burns into "blackened bricks—charred corpses," Kobotsky and Lieb embrace, kiss each other, and part forever.

Love redeems the suffering of Sobel in "The First Seven Years." Sobel, the lonely concentration camp survivor, works as an assistant to Feld, the shoemaker, for 'stingy wages' for five long years only with the hope of marrying his daughter, Miriam. As Feld has other plans for her, Sobel quits the job. Learning Sobel's love for his daughter, Feld asks Sobel to wait for two years till she is twenty-one. Sobel agrees and continues to pound 'leather for love' (20). The confrontation between the shoemaker and his assistant, and the eventual reconciliation, has been called 'pure Malamud,' his special province being "a meeting in which the denied self begins, in pity, to leak past one's guard and for a decisive moment pours forth in a sanctified stream."[48] Besides being a realistic portrayal of the hardships of the immigrant Jews in America, "The First Seven Years" is equally concerned with the mysteries of human heart, and ultimately with the miracle that is wrought by love. Sobel is cast in the mould of Frank Alpine in *The Assistant.*

The story "The Magic Barrel" concerns with the selection of a bride for Leo Finkle, a rabbinical student in the Yeshiva University in New York. Having been advised by a friend that he would have a better congregation if he were married, Leo calls in Pinye Salzman, the marriage-broker, and a luftmensch, for he lives on 'thin air.' Leo recognizes the significance of a marriage-broker in the Jewish history, for he "made practical the necessary without hindering joy" (194). The matchmaker shuffles out a packet of cards from his bag, and selects six of those for Leo's examination. He seeks to impress Leo with the abundance of material possession: "You wouldn't believe me how much cards I got in my office. . . . The drawers are already filled to the top, so I keep them in a barrel, but is every girl good for new rabbi?" (195). In superlatives, he introduces the girl in each picture, and invariably refers to his own life to banish Leo's fears. The first is a widow, and second older in age, but chimes in Pinye, "My own wife is seven year older than me. So what did I suffer?—no, nothing. If Rothschild's daughter wants to marry you, would you say on account of her age, no?" (197). Leo's depression at the failure of a suitable match is conveyed in these words: "All day he ran around in the woods—missed an important appointment, forgot to give out his laundry, walked out of a Broadway cafeteria without paying and had to run back with the ticket in hand; had even not recognized his landlady in the street when she passed with a friend." (194) Next morning the matchmaker again appears, corrects the age of one client, Lily Hirschorn, a high school teacher and catalogues her virtues. Leo meets the girl and whines at being looked upon as a 'passionate prophet.' He later reflects over the subject of loving God, and confesses that, apart from his parents, he hardly cares for anyone:

> Or perhaps it went the other way, that he did not love God so well as he might, because he had loved man. It seemed to Leo that His whole life stood starkly revealed and he saw himself for the first time as he truly was—unloved and loveless. This bitter but somehow not fully unexpected revelation brought him to a point of panic, controlled only by extraordinary effort. He covered his face with his hands and cried. (180)

It is this search for human love from a girl who would treat him as a man and not as a 'semi-mystical Wonder Rabbi' that makes him tell the matchmaker: "Love, I have said to myself, should be a by-product of living and worship rather than its own end. Yet for myself I find it necessary to establish the level of my need and fulfill it" (178). After this inner awakening, Leo picks up the long-neglected packet that Pinye had left with him. He abruptly notices one snapshot that seizes his mind. He wants to know about this girl, Pinye says, "She is not for you. She is a wild one—wild, without shame. This is not a bride for a rabbi" (184). He later lets out that the sinful girl is his daughter, Stella. Leo is now determined in his goal and he insists on meeting her. At times suspecting that Pinye had designed it to happen that way, Leo goes to meet Stella with a small bouquet of violet and rose-buds. Though he sees her smoking by the lamp post and wearing white with red shoes, her eyes are filled with 'desperate innocence' and the pictures in them his 'own redemption.' This moment is rendered symbolically: "Violence and lit candles revolved in the sky. Leo ran forward with flowers out thrust," and the story ends on this note: "Around the corner, Salzman, leaning against a wall, chanted prayers for the dead" (188).

The thematic thrust in the story upholds Malamud's belief in the value of human love which only later can lead to love of God. Loving mankind involves a conscious acknowledgement of its moral infirmities and dark patches, otherwise knowledge about God would remain superficial, mere empty rhetoric without the animating spirit.

In the collection, *The Magic Barrel*, Malamud describes the anguish of the disinherited and the injured bakers, shoemakers, tailors, grocers and matchmakers. He also captures their inarticulate idiom of human credentials. Most of them are fugitives from the holocaust of tyranny and injustice and they spin their fantasies about a better order of life. They know that the price of aspiration is invariably suffering, still, the bargain is worthwhile, for this would be the only evidence of being a Feld, a Kessler, a Lieb and a Panessa. In Malamud's vision, the meaning and depth of life are comprehended through a critical awareness of one's potentials. Malamud seems to suggest through these fables in *The Magic Barrel* his perception of human imperfection and the possibility of an unspectacular control over the forces of moral disintegration.

The second collection of short stories *Idiots First* invests the Malamudian *Schlemiel* with "dignity as well as pathos."[49] Malamud's compassion for the suffering protagonists redeems the stories of ensnarement "from being merely oppressive."[50] Herbert Leibowitz writes:

> Malamud is sort of waggish minstrel of misery. He is a homilist whose stock of canny folk proverbs contains the distilled wisdom of the politic of survival. Since his characters usually live in a kind of psychic jails, they defend their self-respect by crying out in protest against an unhearing, uncaring, world; by laughing, wailing, groaning, or shouting threats at the bullying powers that balk them.[51]

Here, in these short stories Malamud means to have extended his area of observation as he involves his characters with the gross actualities of the world. He is conscious of insistent compulsion on the individual than his private pain and nostalgic memories. While the title story stresses the redemptive value of compassion, stories like "The Death of Me," "The German Refugee" and "The Cost of Living" speak out for compassion in the wake of violence and depression. It would be appropriate to believe that *Idiots First* confronts the reader "with a reconstructionist view of society and man's position in it."[52]

The story "Life Is Better than Death" turns upon the consequences of a spouse's sexual betrayal. When Armando Etta Oliva's husband left her to resume his affair with a cousin, Etta fell to her knees and prayed for his death. Her murderous prayer seemed to have been answered, "the sleeping Armando rolled out of the back of the truck bringing him back to the cousin in Perugia and 'was dead before he stopped rolling.'"[53] Believing that she caused his death, Etta is consumed with guilt. Consequently she starts visiting his grave. There, she meets Cesare Montaldi, a free-lance journalist, who also comes to mourn at the grave of his spouse who was killed while hurrying to meet a lover. Cesare discreetly argues that she was not the cause of Armando's death. Cesare presents his argument; "If Our Lord Himself this minute let Armando rise from the dead to take up his life on earth, tonight—he would be lying in his cousin's bed" (99). Though Etta cries, she recognises the truth of Cesare's remark. Her sexual desire reawakened, she sleeps with him the next time they meet. Etta separates her life and her husband's death. When she tells Cesare that she is pregnant, her lover reassures her that creation of life is not to be regretted, and he will take responsibility of the child. However, Cesare disappears and Etta mourns the loss of Cesare and "the life in her belly" (100). She returns to thinking of herself as an adulteress, but this time one who no longer has the right to return to Armando's grave. Now, Etta considers herself married to a dead man, the effect she had towards one or both men has been displaced towards the organism growing within her.

In these short stories, Malamud explores further his humanistic territory. In Mendel's anxiety for the welfare of Issac, in Nat's affirmation of one 'human color' in Sam's dreams of happiness, and in Maurice's definition of tragedy and 'a rich life,' we recognize the nuances in the Malamudian voice, the voice of the secular human heart. If a Marcus and a Josip had learnt to coexist, if a Cronin could love a once-fallen woman, if a Cesare were honest in his declaration of love, if a Harry could be compassionate towards the disadvantaged, if an Orlando were not deceived, and if an Oskar were not a fugitive, life would have been more powerful. The very fact that Malamud examines the pathos of imperfection and the trauma of betrayal suggest that he is as conscious of human infirmities as of man's capacity to be kind and magnanimous. In all these gloomy situations, Malamud suggests that "unless love balances, the bleak negativism of the Law . . . there can be no rebirth, no triumph of the spirit against egotism and evil."[54]

After *Idiots First*, Malamud published *Pictures of Fidelman: An Exhibition* that "contains five previously published stories and one new story."[55] These stories deal with misadventures of

Fidelman who comes to Europe in search of both vocation and love. In the first story "Last Mohican," Fidelman comes to Italy and attracts trouble right upon his arrival in the form of Simon Susskind. It is Simon Susskind "the last honest man, honest to art and to conscience"[56] and also mysterious refugee, a wandering Jew of desperate needs, who acts as the catalytic character to bring Fidelman to realize his responsibility to fellowmen and to others.

In the story "Still Life," having realized the futility of his pursuit of art-history, Fidelman returns to painting. His sexual adventures and failures with a neurotic woman, Annamaria Olivoino evokes grotesque humour. Enticed by the advertisement of Olivoino, Fidelman joins her studio for rent. The love-making of Fidelman and Annamaria attains ridiculous lengths due to frequent disturbances as usual in Malamud's stories. Even after his failure in love, Fidelman does not stop courting Annamaria. He cringes further to do the most abominable services to her. Annamaria's invitation to a party makes Fidelman happy in his depression. When Annamaria and Balducci enter into a contest of painting a male nude Fidelman readily agrees to do modelling, hoping that it would arouse her interest. But his hopes are belied. Annamaria wants to sleep with Balducci and cruelly orders Fidelman out of her sight. Through Fidelman's situation, Malamud "challenges the last remnant of the hero-myth in the Western culture, the myth of the artist as the final embodiment of that noble quest for purity and truth."[57] Fidelman is quite like Prufrock in his inability to make any progress with his ladylove. Moreover, his tragedy like Roy Hobbs in *The Natural* is that though he is capable of love, he tends to bestow it on unworthy women.

The story "Glass Blower of Venice" has Fidelman emerging from the "underworld of the tortured self."[58] He gives up painting and makes both ends meet by performing menial errands. Having accepted his limitations, Fidelman tries to make sense out of life without illusions and evasions. He, now, seeks his true identity by turning down all the false identities (as an art critic and as an artist). In Malamud's fiction, the experience of failure is "simply the testing ground of character, its purpose is to explore the possibilities for moral development and spiritual regeneration which follow from a recognition of the fact of failure."[59] Fidelman fails and his essential potential to be a better human proves not in any heroic action, but in his recognition of his failure as an artist.

Moreover, we have noticed Malamud's "reluctance to give upon anyone. Each being unique, responsible and redeemable. None is beyond redemption, and in most instances love is the surest means of attaining it."[60] Love is the ultimate, permanent and true value in Malamud's novels of successful quest. Fidelman, the selfish critic, imposter, forger, pimp, and Judas learns at last to give love instead of always taking it. With Margherita, he experiences his first long liaison of his life. His relationship with women so far in the novel was functional but his relationship with Margherita is instinctual; it is not his lust that derives him to pursue her. Thus, "by changing his attitude to the respective claims of self and others he enters on his second life, the real new life."[61] Moreover, in Malamud's world, the amount of love a hero willingly gives to others marks the amount of grace life will grant him.

Not finding everything he seeks in Margherita, Fidelman lets himself be taken over by Beppo who initiates him into homosexual love so that for the first time Fidelman says, "I love you," without reservation. "Think of love" the glass blower murmured. "You've run from it all your life. He stopped running."[62] Fidelman learns as S. Levin in *A New Life* has learnt that "the main source of conscious morality was love of life, everybody's life."[63] There is the suggestion of outrage, salvation through sodomy (Beppo), but Malamud wants to jolt us only enough to wake us up. "Malamud is writing about love; and love, which is 'normal' is not an automatic thing like hetero-sexuality. . . . Fidelman's submission to Beppo symbolizes his acceptance of imperfection in existence. Craft and art, love of men and women, not love"[64] in the subject of this picturesque episode. Beppo completes the lesson Susskind had begun. Just as Susskind had destroyed his 'lifeless' first chapter on Giotto, Beppo slashes up all of Fidelman's canvases, saying no art is better than bad art: "It's for your own sake. Show who's master of your fate—bad art or you" (134). Beppo's advice to Fidelman is simply: "If you can't invent art, invent life" (135), and he leads Fidelman "to the recognition of who he is: not the critic of Giotto, not the painter . . . but the craftsman whose art is the product of the spontaneous response to life, and who is thereby enabled to bridge Yeats's division and achieve 'perfection' in life and work."[65]

Apprenticed to Beppo, both lover and spiritual father, Fidelman learns to blow glass—a wonderfully flexible medium. Its flexibility helps Fidelman understand "the possibilities of life" (136). Fidelman, "assisting for love's sake" (137), works for the first time in his life, instructed. In Malamud's fiction, to be apprentice, ready to be tutored about life, carries much moral weight.

Slowly and painfully, Fidelman learns to master the craft till ultimately, just before he leaves Italy for America, Fidelman does manage to produce one perfect red glass bowl. Having learnt the craft of glass blowing and the art of love, Fidelman leaves Beppo, his lover and master, in acceptance of Margherita's desire that he does not break up her family life. He shows his responsibility towards the two people he has loved by going to America where "he worked as a craftsman in glass and loved men and women" (140).

Fidelman's love for men and women is in no way a degeneration of his character: it is less an acceptance of homosexuality than an affirmation of unselfish love for all humanity. Thus, once more, the Malamud hero, by the end of the story, shows sign of self-transcendence. Fidelman has had to learn to accept the failure of his former concept of a new life of personal satisfaction and uninvolvement. In this collection of short stories, Malamud focusses on present-day reality. The simplistic optimism of the earlier novels is discarded by Malamud and a near pessimistic picture of degeneration is painted so as to persuade us to realize the restorative power of love. Love, therefore, is crucial in Malamud's world. The theme of love is presented more through implication than through statement or through climactic development, thus making the theme both effective and interesting. The emancipation from illusion that one finally notices in Fidelman, one can also identify in the chastened egoism of Roy Hobbs, in the mellowed passion of Frank Alpine, in the dramatic gestures of S. Levin, and in the tempered fortitude of Yakov Bok.

In his last collection of short stories *Rembrandt's Hat*, Malamud "continues his concern with the growth or collapse of the fine bond of compassion that binds two human beings together."[66] While the quest for love and compassion appear in the foreground in *The Magic Barrel*, it tends to be implicit and suggestive in *Rembrandt's Hat*. *The Wasteland* theme serves as a subtle pointer to the need for love in *Rembrandt's Hat*. The characters here fail to communicate with each other, and Malamud seems to suggest that communication is the minimum sign of interpersonal responsibility and understanding which are the bases of love and compassion. Stories like "Talking Horse," "The Letter" and "My Son the Murderer" graphically depict the chasm of failure of communication in an anxiety-ridden world, leading to absurd situations.

The title story "Rembrandt's Hat" is an interesting tale of misunderstanding. The art-historian Arkin's innocent comparison of the sculptor Rubin's white cap with "Rembrandt's Hat" develops a fissure between them. Rubin not only stops wearing the hat, but also consciously avoids Arkin. Arkin is at loss to know the cause of Rubin's misunderstanding and hates Rubin for hating him. When his own white-cap presented to him by a student is missing, he suspects Rubin. But the veil of misunderstanding is cleared with his discovery that Rembrandt's hat does not resemble Rubin's. Arkin feels that Rubin's misery is complicated because of his poor accomplishment in sculpture. He immediately apologizes to Rubin for the wrong remark. Thereafter they become friends again. Rubin once again wears his 'Rembrandt's Hat,' "a crown of failure and hope."[67] Malamud suggests here that all misunderstanding can be cleared with proper communication, sympathy and love. Malamud writes, "like a fellow member of the human community and although much of his most memorable work uses fantasy or folk tale motifs, his work is broadly realistic. His aim is the traditional aim of realists—to broaden and deepen the readers' sympathies so that as they learn to understand and lovingly accept the characters, so they will perforce bring enlarged understanding and sympathy to their human encounters in life."[68]

In Malamud's fiction, compassion, love and understanding, rather than physical circumstances, give meaning to one's life. Out of everyday defeats and indignities of ordinary people, Malamud creates beautiful parables that capture the joy as well as the pain of life. In his tragi-comic parables of human pain and possibility, Malamud demonstrates a commitment to suffering human beings in their painfully absurd conditions. No matter how pathetic or foolish, the individual can assert his humanity. Self-transcendence is the ideal which controls much of the character development in his fiction. His characters begin as egocentric, frustrated individuals with an insecurity-dominated need for success and status. They seek sterile satiety of their lust rather than true love relationship. Consequently, self-transcendence becomes a painful process, and it involves a great deal of suffering, usually connected in some way to an elaborate and ritualistic trial by love. This trial by love eventually forces Malamud's protagonists into an intense self-scrutiny in which they begin to realize both their past mistakes and their need to be concerned for others.

## NOTES

1. Jonathan Baumbach, "The Economy of Love: The Novels of Bernard Malamud," *Kenyon Review*, 25: 3 (Summer 1963) 43.
2. *Ibid.*, 439.
3. Qtd. Marcus Klein, "Bernard Malamud: The Sadness of Goodness," *After Alienation: American Novel in Mid-Century* (New York: The World Publishing Company, 1965) 256.
4. Charles Alva Hoyt, "Bernard Malamud and the New Romanticism," *Contemporary American Novelists*, ed. Herry T. Moore (Carbondale: Southern Illinois Univ. Press, 1964) 79.
5. Bernard Malamud, *The Natural* (Harmondsworth: Penguin, 1967) 108.

6. Ruth B. Mandel, "Bernard Malamud's *The Assistant* and *A New Life*: Ironic Affirmation," *Critique* (Winter 1964-1965) 112.
7. Tony Tanner, *City of Words: American Fiction 1950-1970* (New York: Harper and Row, 1971) 325.
8. Sidney Richman, *Bernard Malamud* (New York: Twayne, 1966) 39.
9. *Ibid.*, 35.
10. Ihab Hassan, "The Victim: Images of Evil in Recent American Fiction," *College English*, 21 (December 1959) 144.
11. Granville Hicks, "His Hope on Human Heart," 32.
12. Ruth B. Mandel, 113.
13. Bernard Malamud, *The Assistant* (Harmondsworth: Penguin, 1967) 42.
14. Tony Tanner, "Bernard Malamud and the New Life," *Critical Quarterly*, 10 (Spring-Summer 1968) 157.
15. Bernard Malamud, *A New Life* (New York: Avon, 1980) 17.
16. Nona Balakin, ed., *The Creative Present: Notes on Contemporary American Fiction* (New York: Doubleday, 1963) 224.
17. *Ibid.*, 83.
18. Baumbach, 442.
19. Sidney Richman, 92.
20. Burton Raffel, "Bernard Malamud," *The Literary Review*, 12: 2 (Winter 1969) 153.
21. Bernard Malamud, *The Fixer* (Harmondsworth: Penguin, 1966) 49.
22. Marcus Klein, 15.
23. Gerald Hoag, "Malamud's Trial: *The Fixer* and the Critics," *Western Humanities Review*, 24: 1 (Winter 1970) 11.
24. Steven G. Kellman, "Tenants in the House of Fiction," *Studies in the Novel*, 8: 4 (Winter 1967) 459.
25. Bernard Malamud, *The Tenants* (Harmondsworth: Penguin, 1971) 147.
26. Qtd. Ihab Hassan, "Bernard Malamud: 1976 Fictions within Our Fiction," Richard Astro and Jackson J. Benson, ed., *The Fiction of Bernard Malamud* (Cornvallis: Oregon State University Press, 1977) 56.
27. Ben Siegal, "Through a Glass Darkly: Bernard Malamud's Painful Views of the Self," Richard Astro and Jackson J. Benson, ed., 119.
28. Richard Gilman, "*Dubin's Lives*," *New Republic* (March 24, 1979) 29.

29. Robert Rubenstein, "Search for Self," *The Progressive*, 43 (June 1979) 58.
30. Jackson J. Benson, "An Introduction: Bernard Malamud and Haunting of America," *The Fiction of Bernard Malamud*, 15.
31. Peter S. Prescott, "*A New Life*," *Newsweek* (February 12, 1979) 83.
32. *Ibid.*, 84.
33. Dean Flower, "Picking Up the Pieces," *The Hudson Review*, 32: 2 (Summer 1979) 305.
34. Ralph Tyler, "A Talk with the Novelist," *New York Times Book Review*, 84 (February 18, 1979) 32.
35. Bernard Malamud, *Dubin's Lives* (Harmondsworth: Penguin, 1979) 246.
36. Mark Shechner, "The Return of the Repressed," *The Nation*, 228 (March 19, 1979) 277.
37. *Ibid.*, 279.
38. Marcus Klein, 253.
38. Bernard Malamud, *God's Grace* (Harmondsworth: Penguin, 1982) 17.
39. Robert Alter, "*God's Grace*: A Theological Fantasy," *New Republic*, 187 (September 1982) 39.
40. Clive Sinclaire, "The Falling-Out in Paradise," *Times Literary Supplement* (October 29, 1982) 1188.
41. *Ibid.*
42. Bonnie Lyons, "The Contrasting Visions of Malamud and O'Conner," *Studies in American-Jewish Literature*, 12 (1993) 80.
43. Granville Hicks, 32.
44. Henry Popkin, "Jewish Stories," *Kenyon Review*, 20: 4 (Autumn 1958) 641.
45. R.C. Blackman, "Bernard Malamud," *Christian Science Monitor* (May 15, 1958) 11.
46. Bernard Malamud, *The Magic Barrel* (Harmondsworth: Penguin, 1968) 130.
47. Sidney Richman, 102.
48. David Boroff, "Losers, But not Lost," *Saturday Review* (October 12, 1963) 33.
49. Robert Alter, "Out of the Trap," *Midstream*, 9 (December 4, 1963) 88.
50. Herbert Leibowitz, "Malamud and the Anthropomorphic Business," *New Republic*, 149: 25 (December 21, 1963) 21.

51. Samuel Irving Bellman, "Women, Children and *Idiots First*: Transformation Psychology," *Malamud and the Critics*, 15.
52. Bernard Malamud, *Idiots First* (New York: Farrar, Straus and Giroux, 1963) 94.
53. Herbert Leibowitz, 22.
54. Sheldon J. Harshinow, *Bernard Malamud* (New York: Frederick Unger, 1980) 77.
55. Samuel I. Bellman, 130.
56. Ruth R. Wisse, *The Schlemiel as Modern Hero* (Chicago: Univ. of Chicago Press, 1971) 114.
57. Robert Duchmare, *Art and Idea in the Novels of Bernard Malamud: Towards "The Fixer"* (The Hague: Mouton, 1974) 139.
58. Giles B. Gunn, "Bernard Malamud and the High Cost of Living," *Adversity and Grace: Studies in Recent American Literature*, ed. Nathan Scott Jr. (Chicago: Univ. of Chicago Press, 1968) 65.
59. Ben Siegel, 60.
60. Tony Tanner, 333.
61. Bernard Malamud, *Pictures of Fidelman: An Exhibition* (Harmondsworth: Penguin, 1969) 135.
62. Bernard Malamud, *A New Life*, 237.
63. Robert Scholars, "Portrait of Artist as 'Escape Goat,'" *Saturday Review*, 52 (May 10, 1969) 33.
64. Christof Wegelin, "The American *Schlemiel* Abroad: Malamud's Italian Stories and the End of American Innocence," *Twentieth Century Literature*, 19 (January 1973) 80.
65. Jeffrey Helterman, *Understanding Bernard Malamud* (South Carolina: University of South Carolina Press, 1985) 125.
66. Bernard Malamud, *Rembrandt's Hat* (Harmondsworth: Penguin, 1973) 141.
67. Bonnie Lyons, 81.

# Conclusion

This study demonstrates that the struggle for recognition and acceptance is one of the most important motivational forces of Bernard Malamud's heroes. Notwithstanding some differences, the conception of authenticity and the means by which they achieve it, are similar in nature. Initially, an accurate appraisal of the totality of human condition, that is to say, one's commitment to one's own self consists of craving for external recognition either in the form of love and fame or social position. Eventually, it leads the protagonist to experience a coherent sense of self defined by a code of values. "The underlying paradigm in Bernard Malamud's novels is the universal archetypal heroic journey, which in itself reflects the problematic relationship between self and society. . . . All the heroes from Roy Hobbs in *The Natural* (1952) to Calvin Cohn in *God's Grace* (1982) are concerned with the search for a new identity and with the search for individual and social responsibility."[1] The successful protagonists in Malamud's fiction undergo a process of inner transformation that ultimately allows them to reconcile their hard-won identity with a personal commitment to others.

At first in the course of his pursuit of individual happiness and freedom, the protagonist wishes to remain unscathed and unentangled. His ambition is of a materialistic nature, selfish and inconsiderate towards others. Involvements incur responsibilities that he is not ready to accept for he fears that it will curtail his freedom. He desperately struggles to retain his freedom, however, he is gradually made to face upto freedom's restrictions. For Malamud, it would seem, "human freedom is perhaps illusory, but not commitment to life."[2] In Malamud's fiction, freedom comes from responsibility but not responsibility from freedom. Malamud believes that true freedom lies in not the rejection but the acceptance of binding commitments and relationships. In his world, the "demands of responsibility are tremendous, particularly since they cannot be set forth by a rigid code of ethics, but they impinge upon only a very contracted range of human relationships, particularly upon the relationships between lovers and between parents and children."[3]

In Malamud's world of interpersonal relationships, a new free life is not to be found in a new place but in a new free self developed through a rewarding relationship with others. It is through meaningful relationship in which the need of the 'other' gains priority over the needs of the self, that the protagonist grows in awareness and he struggles to lead a fuller life. In fact, a part of the hero's quest for a new life has been the search for an authentic spiritual father through whose instigation self-recognition comes. It results in a hopeful struggle towards moral growth. The spiritual father alone leads the hero to his goal by teaching him the necessity of discarding his egoistic self-centredness and assuming a responsible role towards others. The basis of the hero's success or failure is his choice of his spiritual father and the acceptance and practice of the values presented in the father figure. Furthermore, the hero must willingly assume fatherhood and the responsibility associated with parenthood. The hero's assumption of parenthood, his willing involvement in the lives of others is indicative of his moral growth.

Malamud shows a concern with situations which generate strong feelings such as of guilt, love and pity in the protagonist. What arouses such feelings in the hero is a new relationship he may have cultivated himself but which is more often implicated upon him against his desires. However, as the hero's involvement grows, the difference also diminishes. We see in Malamud's fiction the hero torn by desires that are contradictory to his conscience, and a conscience in disharmony with the desires. We have then a hero victimized by a self-destructive struggle between high aspirations and low lusts, the incompatible demands of the ethical and the erotic nature.

The protagonist's future possibilities rest upon realization of the contradictory drives within himself and wilful choice between the fulfilment of selfish desires and selfless commitment towards others. Gradually he is made to realize that within himself are the qualities that nullify his struggle for authenticity and face up to the conflicting demands of his moral and materialistic self. His decision to confront himself and change for the better leads to the movement from self-regard towards selfless commitment and ultimate affirmation of the values Malamud has always propagated. Through a painful process, the protagonist changes himself and his priorities so as to make him worthy of a new life of value. In Malamud's world, anything of value is not easily acquired—it has to be earned and it is at the cost of materialistic aspirations that the protagonist gains moral insight.

Malamud firmly believes that people can change and become better human beings in spite of the denigrating conditions of life. He says, "A man is always changing and the changing part of him is all-important. I refer to the psyche, to the spirit, the mind, the emotions."[4] In this change to the better lies the hope and promise of a better future for the protagonist.

The degree of transcendence between Malamud's protagonists varies according to the degree of personal affirmation each makes. Nonetheless, all heroes move from withdrawal to commitment, from selfishness to selflessness and assert their humanity through compassion towards others. Graduating from egoistic desires to love and responsibility towards others opens the hero to more meaningful relationships and through them to newer possibilities and a new way of life.

Each of Malamud's novels is concerned with the hero's decision to seek a new life. The quest takes him on a journey into self. Before Malamud's hero can realize his desperate hope of living with others, he must live with himself. At first, we see a person trying to live by unfulfillable notions of himself. However, through experience and self-analysis he, in time, learns the necessary lessons of self-denial. He grows in heroic stature as he accommodates to the needs of others, but such heroism is also the hero's loss for he has to sacrifice his personal desires in favour of the needs of others. Eventually, he earns a free self but one quite different from the one he had envisioned at the onset of his quest. By the end he has learnt painful lessons and has matured to the point where he can fully accept his own imperfections and the reality of his situation without recourse to the fictions and illusions that had earlier ruled his life. Having gained an awareness of himself and the world, there is at least a thin chance that his future will be a little less painful than his past. By now, he has learnt that "it is in striving that the self exists and not in the end, not in the realized goal; that man is a becomingness and not being and that in this fact lie his hopefulness and freedom."[5]

Malamud's morality, essentially, means "the necessity in this world of accepting moral obligations."[6] Malamud's hero must not only try to make life better just for himself, he must assume the responsibility of making life better for others even at the cost of his own betterment. There comes the question of affinity between responsibility of suffering. Malamud's protagonist suffers. He is the victim of adverse circumstances, other people's whims and above all his own personal failings. It is his search for materialistic gains and his irresponsible self-centredness that leads to the protagonist's suffering and it is through suffering he achieves self-discipline and learns the value of love, charity and responsibility towards others. In Malamud's fiction, suffering is a test of character.

Malamud takes inordinate interest in the attitude that one should adopt towards suffering, a pre-condition of life—whether one should make it a value or just accept it as a necessary appendage of responsibility that must be tolerated for it is a lesser evil than the alternatives. In his earlier novels, Malamud seemed to invest a moral capital in suffering. Suffering passively seems to be the only way to express self-sacrificial, loving concern for others. He seems to sanction passivity and acquiescence to the injustice of the existentially chaotic world. However, passivity is not explicitly praised as a virtue. Malamud is divided against himself as to the value of suffering. Ambiguity sets in and his attitude towards suffering undergoes a subtle change. Malamud begins to recognize the difference between hopeless suffering caused by injustice and natural suffering which is unavoidable. In his later novels, Malamud openly criticizes the acquiescing passivity that had found favour with the earlier heroes. Suffering without cause has in itself a negative quality. Affirmation does not lie in the masochistic seeking of suffering but in rebellion against unjust suffering. Unlike Dostoevsky, Malamud does not consider suffering as the means of ultimate salvation and the only means of purification.

Nevertheless, whether suffering is of value or not, it is only through suffering that Malamud's heroes grow. It is not the intensity of suffering that interests Malamud, it is what one learns from the experience of suffering once one accepts the inevitability of suffering in one's life that Malamud writes about.

In *The Natural*, Roy suffers again because he denies commitment towards others. Besides he learns no better from suffering. Suffering is to teach us to want right things but Roy never accepts the fact until it is too late. Morris in *The Assistant* best expresses Malamud's theme of the inevitability of suffering: "If you live, you suffer." But what is more important is the right approach to suffering. "I suffer for you," Morris tells Frank, for to be able to suffer for other is not the ill-fate of man but his privilege. In *A New Life*, Levin learns that if he wishes to start afresh and give meaning to his life, he will have to accommodate the possibility of much more suffering in the future than what he has suffered in the past. Indeed it is through suffering that the hero grows in personal maturity. Yakov in *The Fixer* is against suffering but understands the need to make the experience meaningful when both unavoidable and necessary. The hero's quest for a new life only ironically gives the hero the freedom to choose to suffer. In *Pictures of Fidelman: An Exhibition*, Fidelman suffers setbacks in his artistic pursuits because he shirks participating in the suffering of others. In *The Tenants*, it is shared anguish which is the turning point in Lesser's life. It will lead to compassion and responsibility towards others. In *Dubin's Lives*, we see Dubin neglect his family in pursuit of selfish desires and as a consequence suffer physical impotency and mental block. His afflictions come to an end only when he returns to his wife with love.

For Malamud, even a new life is a life rooted in the suffering each hero has undergone in the past. In fact, the hero's struggle for recognition only makes him willingly choose to suffer again—this time for the sake of others. To suffer for the good of others is a redemptive value in Malamud's fiction, participating in the suffering of others adds value to one's life. Suffering is the "good willed and deliberate acknowledgement and acceptance of the common life of man. It is the expression of the way in which men are bound together in their loss."[7]

It is their common fate of ill-luck and suffering which binds Malamud's Jews and his Gentiles; they all suffer frustrations in their materialistic ambitions and carnal desires. Malamud believes that shared suffering unites people and leads to brotherhood and mutual understanding. He has said, "those who want for others must expect to give up something. What we get in return is the affirmation of what we believe in."[8]

Love, like responsibility, is akin to suffering. To love other, given Malamud's imperatives, is to suffer. In other words, suffering binds people in love. "Suffering is the one possibility of love. Therefore, it is morality itself."[9] Thus, in Malamud's metaphysics, suffering is an expression of love and each protagonist learns "what it is like to live by suffering for what one loves—indeed by loving what makes him suffer."[10] Malamud's heroes, the unloved orphans, are in great need of love. It is through love that these imperfect beings learn responsibility and it is only through a commitment to love that they find salvation. The hero's ability to love without selfish motives is his saving grace in Malamud's moral world.

Suffering in Malamud's novels has a peculiar Jewish flavour. Indeed, his fiction shows the hold of past on his psyche—of their familial hardships as poor immigrants, his childhood spent in slums, his maturing years witnessing persecution of the Jews by Hitler in Germany. All this led to Malamud's realization of the martyrdom of the Jews throughout history. He writes of the Jewish experience but in such a way that it comes to stand for the experience of all modern men. "The Jewish experience as is known to all, refers to their profound suffering and known to all, refers to their profound suffering and meaningless persecution."[11]

The suffering, alienation and exile characterizing the Jew's experience for two thousand years become in modern times everyone's condition in the American culture and offers the Jew as a symbol of the modern predicament.

Malamud's hero draws his moral perspective from the painful experiences of the historical Jew who suffered centuries of persecution but did not lose his dignity or his humanity. For Malamud, the Jew symbolizes the alienated individual who in spite of his existential anguish has the ability to learn selfless commitment towards others and thus pave his way to moral transcendence. As Solotaroff puts it, "Malamud's Jewishness is a type of metaphor for anyone's life—both, for the tragic dimensions of anyone's life and for a code of personal morality and salvation that is more psychological than religious."[12]

The Jew with his humanity represents the hopes and possibilities of the twentieth century caught in the horrors of the Holocaust. Malamud's work is, in a way, a tribute to his race. With Jewishness he associates the best qualities in man—goodness, charity, kindness and sympathy, moreover, he seeks the Jew in every man. In Malamud's fiction, to be a Jew is the same as to be a Christian for both insist on doing "What is right, to be honest, to be good."[13] Malamud writes about Jews but does not highlight his Jew's religious or ethnic identity. His Jew is an individual whose Jewishness lies in his qualities of suffering and endurance, and it is this Jewishness that Malamud universalizes. Malamud's Jewish characters are real, not inventions, "fully realized fictional characters whose experiences have meaning and impact on a direct personal level as on a universal or metaphorical level."[14] To deny one's Jewishness is to deny one's humanity. Malamud's ultimate preoccupation is essentially with humanity. The hero's particular experience is universal.

Malamud's theme of suffering is closely linked with his use of mythic method. Malamud uses the ancient myths as a device, apt for emphasizing the necessity of preserving traditional values, which is contrasted with his use of the American Dream

Myth with its "tawdry values of a new world commercial optimism."[15] Everyone of Malamud's heroes is caught in the myth of the American Dream that sanctions all materialistic values. In Malamud's world, the hero can find spiritual fulfilment only if he adopts the traditional values of unselfish love and responsibility as propounded in the ancient myths. Of this tension Walter Shear says, "for the characters these two systems of values become burdens, handicaps, imposers of demands which they cannot meet most frequently because these demands pull them in opposite directions. Both these value worlds are embodied in all the characters."[16] Caught in this cultural conflict, the problem of identity looms large in the hero's mind. It is not a problem faced only by Jews, it is every man's dilemma. "Man, caught between the conflicting claims of cultural values, suffers not only because of his circumstances but because the fragmented abundance of the worldviews produce uncertainty about intentions, actions and roles,"[17] further says Walter Shear. The ordeal of the mythic hero inevitably involves suffering and pain.

Malamud's use of the mythic archetypes as a structural device to highlight the theme shows a marked improvement with Malamud's growing art. Malamud's first novel *The Natural* makes a naive use of myth for it controls the theme of *The Natural*, making the hero act according to the dictates of his mythic role. But from *The Assistant* onwards, there is no externally imposed mythic system which governs the action of the characters. Myth forms the backdrop of the theme and is used with admirable discretion and subtlety.

Symbols, like myths, have been used by Malamud as a structural device to celebrate his theme of regeneration. The most pervasive symbol in his fiction is that of a 'prison.' Firstly, the prison forms a perfect metaphor for the human and the Jewish condition of alienation, withdrawal and suffering. However, not only are Malamud's heroes victimized by fate and imprisoned by circumstances, they are, above all, prisoners of their own imperfect selves. Imprisoned in dark, dingy general stores and old tenements, they are bound by their own limited selves. They isolate themselves through their intolerance towards others and make prisons for themselves their selfishness. They are caught and restrained by their own personal failings and the limitations that life imposes on them. Thus Malamud's most common motif of imprisonment is a symbol of an underdeveloped self unable to reach out to others.

To break out of the prison, the protagonist must not only accept his own personal limitations, he must transcend them. Working within the barriers life imposes, he must burst his bonds. "The impression is of an imagination working through the entrapments of art or money or sex or guilt or race—pressing always towards liberation into some universal human space."[18] The protagonist can gain freedom by breaking out of his own egoistic self, reaching out to others in selfless commitment and adopting a humane approach to life.

It is freedom of the inner self which is the thematic problem of Malamud's fiction. He says: "I was very much interested in the idea of prison as a source of the self's freedom," and, "a man has to construct, invent his freedom."[19] Freedom, obviously, for Malamud, does not mean simply being physically unrestrained; it is an attitude towards life that allows one to make the best of one's circumstances.

Integral to Malamud's theme and vision are humour and irony. The hero's painful initiation into his new life is somewhat relieved by the comic efforts of the *Schlemiel* hero to succeed in life. "Laughter serves in the capacity of a redemptive emotion; it is a reminder that the way of transcendence lies only through the ability to endure privation,"[20] writes Sidney Richman. Ironically comic, the characters can laugh at themselves and escape from their painful existence. The mixture of pain, irony and humour strikes one note over and over again—of compassion. His heroes are comic victims at whom we laugh yet associate ourselves within their search for authenticity. It is a serious search conducted with comic bungling. Moreover, humour in Malamud's fiction is an ironic technique that projects both the existentially absurd reality of everyday life and helps sustain hope in affirmation through the values of humanism.

Malamud's ironic perspective gives him objectivity and distance in dealing with the material he otherwise feels wholly involved with. His touch of irony saves him from sentimentality but he blends his irony with a degree of compassion which makes his portrayal of the Jews very realistic. He has an ironic yet compassionate insight into the lives of his little people. In his fiction, irony works by creating a distance between the reality of the situation and the dream world of freedom that the hero creates for himself. His deft use of irony projects the ambiguity of life and underscores the contrast between chaotic, dehumanizing reality and the aspirations that are humane. Malamud blends compassion with irony to delineate his protagonist's dilemma. Justifying the ironic technique, Ruth Mandel says, "It is the disparity between hopes, dreams and aspirations of the characters in the novel and the horrible reality that is insisted upon over and over again. . . . This shocking and repeated juxtaposition of hope and reality is the essential part of the ironic technique."[21]

It is irony and affirmation, worldly defeat and spiritual hope which define the Malamudian hero's predicament. Disillusioned with his dreams, he is still not completely crushed. He eventually learns to look within himself for source of freedom and moral growth. His success in his quest, qualified to the maximum, is partial. This is because his quest for freedom as well as for love is in itself contradictory. It has seeds of both denial and affirmation. Seeking freedom would mean unwillingness to take on responsibility of others while the quest for love can only be fulfilled if one accepts suffering and responsibility of others.

Malamud's fiction is not depressive or gloomy nor does he write out of bitterness. Quite on the contrary, he writes with full faith in mankind and with love and compassion for human failings in this imperfect world. By presenting the apparently infructuous, disorderly lives his protagonists lead, Malamud makes us aware of the modern man's dilemma and drives home the need for universal love and brotherhood more forcefully. In spite of the discouraging reality of the surface story, Bernard Malamud constantly reaffirms his faith in human values and man's ability to achieve authenticity, acceptance and recognition.

# NOTES

1. Pirjo Ahokas, "Through the Ghetto to Giotto: The Process of Inner Transformation in Malamud's 'Last Mohican,'" *American Studies in Scandinavia*, 19 (1987) 57.
2. Robert L. White, "Two Novels by Roth and Malamud," *Forum*, 4 (Winter 1963) 21.
3. *Ibid.*
4. W.J. Handy, "The Malamud Hero: A Quest for Existence," Richard Astro and Jackson J. Benson, ed., *The Fiction of Bernard Malamud* (Cornvallis: Oregon State Univ. Press, 1970) 77.
5. Helen Weinberg, *The New Novel in America: The Kafkan Mode in Contemporary Fiction* (Ithaca: Cornell Univ. Press, 1970) 28.
6. Marcus Klein, *After Alienation: American Novels in Mid-Century* (New York: World Book Publishing Company, 1963) 263.
7. *Ibid.*
8. Daniel Stern, "The Art of Fiction: Bernard Malamud," *Paris Review*, 61 (Spring 1975) 61.
9. Marcus Klein, 263.
10. Gilman B. Gunn, "Bernard Malamud and High Cost of Living," in Nathan A. Scott, Jr., ed., *Adversity and Grace: Studies in Recent American Literature* (Chicago: Univ. of Chicago Press, 1968) 84.
11. Naresh Guha, "Notes on the Importance of Jewish-American Literature," *Indian Essays* (1970) 248.
12. Theodore Solotaroff, "Bernard Malamud's Fiction: The Old Life and the New," *Commentary*, 33 (March 1962) 198.
13. Bernard Malamud, *The Assistant* (Harmondsworth: Penguin, 1963) 113.
14. Robert Ducharme, *Art and Idea in the Novels of Bernard Malamud: Towards "The Fixer"* (The Hague: Mouton, 1974) 93.
15. *Ibid.*, 7.
16. Walter Shear, "Cultural Conflict in *The Assistant*," *Midwest Quarterly*, 7 (Summer 1966) 369.
17. *Ibid.*, 379.
18. Daniel Stern, 54.
19. Sidney Richman, *Bernard Malamud* (New York: Twayne, 1966) 68.
20. *Ibid.*
21. Ruth. B. Mandel, "Bernard Malamud's *The Assistant* and *A New Life*: Ironic Affirmation," *Critique*, 7 (Winter 1964-65) 114.

# Bibliography

## Primary Sources

Malamud, Bernard. *The Natural*. Harmondsworth: Penguin, 1967.

_____. *The Assistant*. Harmondsworth: Penguin, 1967.

_____. *The Magic Barrel and Other Stories*. Harmondsworth: Penguin, 1968.

_____. *A New Life*. New York: Avon, 1980.

_____. *Idiots First*. New York: Farrar, Straus and Giroux, 1963.

_____. *The Fixer*. Harmondsworth: Penguin, 1968.

_____. *Pictures of Fidelman: An Exhibition*. Harmondsworth: Penguin, 1972.

_____. *The Tenants*. Harmondsworth: Penguin, 1971.

_____. *Rembrandt's Hat*. Harmondsworth: Penguin, 1976.

_____. *Dubin's Lives*. Harmondsworth: Penguin, 1979.

_____. *God's Grace*. Harmondsworth: Penguin, 1982.

## Secondary Sources

### Books

Aldridge, John W. *The Contemporary Novel in Crisis*. New York: D. Mckay, 1966.

Alexander, Edward. *The Resonance of Dust: Essays on Holocaust Literature and Jewish Fate*. Columbus: Ohio State Univ. Press, 1979.

Allen, Walter. *The Modern Novel in Britain and the United States*. New York: E.P. Dutton, 1964.

Alter, Robert. *After the Tradition: Essays on Modern Jewish Writing* New York: Dutton, 1969.

Alter, Robert. *Partial Magic: The Novel as a Self-Conscious Genre*. Berkeley: Univ. of California Press, 1975.

Amin, Samir. *Delinking: Towards a Polycentric World*. London: Zed, 1985.

Axthelm, Peter. *The Modern Confessional Novel.* New Haven: Meridian Books, 1967.

Barret, W. *Irrational Man: A Study in Existential Philosophy.* New York: Doubleday, 1958.

Baumbach, Jonathan. *The Landscape of Nightmare: Studies in the Contemporary American Novel.* New York: New York Univ. Press, 1965.

Berger, Alan L. *Crisis and Covenant: The Holocaust in American Jewish Fiction.* Albany: State Univ. of New York Press, 1985.

Bloom, Allen. *The Closing of American Mind.* New York: Simon and Schuster, 1987.

Bradbury, Malcolm. *The Modern American Novel.* Oxford: Oxford Univ. Press, 1983.

Bryant, Jerry H. *The Open Decision: The Contemporary American Novel and its Intellectual Background.* New York: Free Press, 1970.

Burgess, Anthony. *The Novel Now: A Guide to Contemporary Fiction.* New York: Norton, 1967.

Burnett, Whit, ed. *This Is My Best: In the Third Quarter of the Century.* Garden City: Doubleday, 1970.

Charney, Maurice. *Sexual Fiction.* London: Methuen, 1981.

Chase, Richard. *The American Novel and its Tradition.* London: G. Bell and Sons, 1958.

Clifford, James and George E. Marcus. *Writing Culture: The Poetics and Politics of Ethnography.* Berkeley: Univ. of California Press, 1986.

Cohen, Sandy. *Bernard Malamud and the Trial by Love.* Amsterdam: Rodopi N.V., 1974.

Cowley, Malcolm. *Exile's Return: A Literary Odyssey of the 1920s.* New York: Doubleday, 1951.

Demobo, L.S. *The Monological Jew: A Literary Study.* Wisconsin: The Univ. of Wisconsin Press, 1988.

Detweiler, Robert. *Four Spiritual Crises in Mid-Century American Fiction.* Florida: Univ. of Florida Press, 1964.

Diamond Malcohn L. *Martin Buber: Jewish Existentialist.* New York: Oxford Univ. Press, 1960.

Donald, Miles. *The American Novel in the Twentieth Century.* London: Harper and Row, 1978.

Feuerlicht, Ignace. *Alienation: From the Past to the Future.* Westport: Greenwood, 1978.

Fiedler, Leslie A. *Waiting for the End*. New York: Stein and Day, 1964.

______. *No! In Thunder: Essays on Myth and Literature*. New York: Stein and Day, 1972.

______. *To the Gentiles*. New York: Stein and Day, 1972.

Field, Leslie A. and Joyce W. Field, ed. *Bernard Malamud: A Collection of Critical Essays*. New Jersey: Prentice Hall, 1975.

Finkelstein, Sidney. *Existentialism and Alienation in American Literature*. New York: International Publishers, 1965.

Freidman, Maurice. *Problematic Rebel*. Chicago: Univ. of Chicago Press, 1970.

French, Warren. ed. *The Fifties: Fiction, Poetry, Drama*. Deland: Everett and Edwards, 1972.

Freud, Sigmund. *Civilization and Its Discontents*. London: Random House, 1964.

Fuller, Edmund. *Man in Modern Fiction: Some Minority Opinions in Contemporary American Writings*. New York: Random House, 1958.

Geismer, Maxwell. *American Moderns: From Rebellion to Conformity*. New York: Hill and Wang, 1958.

Glazer, Nathan. *American Judaism*. Chicago: Univ. of Chicago Press, 1972.

Glicksberg, Charles I. *Literature and Religion: A Study in Conflict*. Westport: Greenwood Press, 1977.

Gordon, Milton. *Assimilation in American Life*. New York: Oxford Univ. Press, 1964.

Gutmann, Amy. *Multiculturalism: Examining the Politics of Recognition*. New Jersey: Princeton Univ. Press, 1994.

Guttman, Allen. *The Jewish Writer in America: Assimilation and the Crisis of Identity*. New York: Oxford Univ. Press, 1968.

Handy, William J. *Modern Fiction: A Formalist Approach*. Cardondale: Southern Iliinois Univ. Préss, 1971.

Harishinow, Sheldon J. *Bernard Malamud*. New York: Frederick Unger, 1980.

Harrison, Gilbert A. ed. *The Critic as Artist: Essays on Books 1920-1970*. New York: Liveright, 1972.

Hassan, Ihab. *Radical Innocence: Studies in the Contemporary American Novel*. Princeton: Princeton Univ. Press, 1967.

Hay, Peter L. *The Limping Hero: Grotesques in Literature*. New York: New York Univ. Press, 1971.

Hendin, Josephine. *Vulnerable People: A View of American Fiction since 1945*. New York: Oxford Univ. Press, 1978.

Hicks, Granville. *Literary Horizon: A Quarter Century of American Fiction*. New York: New York Univ. Press, 1970.

Hoffman, Frederick J. *The Mortal No: Death and the Modern Imagination*. New Jersey: Princeton Univ. Press, 1964.

Kahn, Joel S. *Culture, Multiculture, Postculture*. London: Sage, 1995.

Keppler, C.F. *The Literature of the Second Self*. Arizona: Univ. of Arizona Press, 1972.

Klein, Marcus. *After Alienation*. Cleveland: World Publishing, 1964.

Knopp, Josephine Zadorsky. *The Trial of Judaism in Contemporary Jewish Writing*. Urbana: Univ. of Illinois Press, 1975.

Kort, Wesley. *Shriven Selves: Religious Problems in Recent American Fiction*. Philadelphia: Fortress Press, 1972.

Kostelanetz, Richard. *The End of Intelligent Writing: Literary Politics in America*. New York: Sheed and Ward, 1974.

Lesher, Lawrence, ed. *Conversations with Bernard Malamud*. Jackson: Univ. Press of Mississippi, 1991.

Liptzin, Soloman. *The Jew in American Literature*. New York: Block, 1966.

Malin, Irving. ed. *Contemporary American Jewish Literature: Critical Essays*. Bloomington: Indiana Univ. Press, 1973.

_____. *Jew and American*. Carbondale: Southern Illinois Press, 1965.

May, Keith M. *Out of the Maelstrom: Psychology and the Novel in the Twentieth Century*. London: Paul Elek, 1977.

Mudrick, Marvin. *On Culture and Literature*. New York: Horizon, 1970.

Munitz, Hilton K. *Identity and Individuation*. New York: New York Univ. Press, 1971.

Nagel, James, ed. *American Fiction: Historical and Critical Essays*. Boston: Northeastern Univ. Press, 1977.

Pinsker, Sanford. *The Schlemiel as Metaphor: Studies in the Yiddish and American Jewish Novel*. Carbondale: Southern Illinois Univ. Press, 1971.

_____. *Between Two Worlds: The American Novel in the 1960s*. New York: The Whitson Publishing Company, 1980.

Podhoretz, Norman. *Doing and Undoing: The Fifties and After in America*. New York: Farrar, Straus and Giroux, 1964.

Rahv, Philip. *Literature and the Sixth Sense*. Boston: Houghton Muffin, 1960.

Rude, Donald, ed. *Alienation: Minority Groups*. New York: John Wiley and Sons, 1972.

Ruotolo, Lucio. *Six Existential Heroes: The Politics of Faith*. Massachusetts: Harvard Univ. Press, 1973.

Rupp, Richard H. *Celebration in Postwar American Fiction 1945-1967*. Florida: Univ. of Miami Press, 1970.

Rutherford, Jonathan, ed. *Identity: Community, Culture, Difference*. London: Lawrence and Wishart, 1990.

Said, Edward. *Culture and Imperialism*. London: Chatto and Windus, 1993.

Scholes, Robert. *Fabulation and Meta-Fiction*. Urbana: Univ. of Illinois Press, 1979.

Schultz, Maz F. *Radical Sophistication: Studies in Contemporary Jewish-American Novelists*. Ohio: Ohio Univ. Press, 1969.

Sherman, Bernard. *The Invention of the Jew: Jewish-American Novelist 1916-1964*. New York: The Omas Yosehold, 1969.

Sherman, C.B. *The Jew within American Society: A Study in Ethnic Individuality*. Chicago: Univ. of Chicago Press, 1961.

Sypher, Wylie. *The Loss of Self in Modern Literature and Art*. New York: Random House, 1961.

Taylor, Charles. *Sources of Self*. Cambridge, MA: Harvard Univ. Press, 1989.

Trilling, Lionel. *Freud and the Crisis of Our Culture*. Boston: Houghton Muffin, 1962.

Weinkerg, Helen. *The New Novel in America: The Kafkan Mode in Contemporary Fiction*. Ithaca: Cornell Univ. Press, 1970.

Young, Iris. *Justice and the Politics of Difference*. Princeton: Princeton Univ. Press, 1990.

Zablocki, Benjamin David. *Alienation and Charisma: A Study of Contemporary American Communes*. New York: The Free Press, 1980.

## Articles

Aarons, Victoria. "The Outsider within: Women in Contemporary Jewish-American Fiction," *Contemporary Literature* 28: 3 (1987) 378-93.

Adams, Phobe. "The Burdens of the Past," *Atlantic* (November 1961) 184-85.

Ahokas, Pirjo. "Through the Ghetto to Giotto: The Process of Inner Transformation in Malamud's 'Last Mohican.'" *American Studies in Scandinavia* 19 (1987) 57-69.

Alexander, Edward. "Race Fever," *Commentary* 90 (1990) 95-102.

Alter, Robert. "Malamud as Jewish Writer," *Commentary* 42 (1966) 71-76.

Angoff, Charles. "How 'Jewish' are Jewish Writers in America?," *Tradition* 16: 2 (1976) 24-34.

Arrowsmith, William. "Literature and the Uses of Anxiety," *Western Humanities Review* 10: 4 (1956) 325-35.

Avery, Evelyn. "Pictures of Malamud," *Studies in American Jewish Literature* 7: 2 (1988) 224-31.

Bailey, Anthony. "Insidious Patience," *Commonweal* 64 (1957) 307-8.

Baris, Sharon Deykin. "Intertextuality and Reader Responsibility: Living on in Malamud's 'The Mourners'," *Studies in American Jewish Literature* 11: 1 (1992) 45-61

Barret, William. "American Fiction and American Values," *Partisan Review* 18: 6 (1951) 681-90.

Bellow, Saul. "Some Notes on Recent American Fiction," *Encounter* 21 (1963) 54-69.

Benedict, Helen. "Bernard Malamud: Morals and Surprises," *The Antich Review* 41: 1 (1983) 28-36.

Berger, Bridgittlee. "Multiculturalism and the Modern University," *Partisan Review* (1993) 31-42.

Bluefarb, Sam. "Bernard Malamud: The Scope of Caricature," *English Journal* 53 (1964) 319-26.

Bouraoui, H.A. "A Quest for Meaning: The Crisis of Awareness," *Journal of Popular Culture* 6 (1972) 363-73.

Buchen, Irving H. "Malamud's *God's Grace*: Divine Genesis, Mortal Terminus," *Studies in American Jewish Literature* 10: 1 (1991) 24-84.

Canham, Laurel. "Matrix and Allegory in Selected Malamud Short Stories," *Linguistic in Literature* 2: 3 (1977) 59-91.

Clark, Suzanne. "Bernard Malamud in Oregon," *American Scholar* 59 (1990) 67-79.

Cottorl, Robert J. "American the Multicultural," *American Educator* 2 (1990) 51-58.

Cronin, Gloria L. "The Complex Irony of Grace: A Study of Bernard Malamud's *God's Grace*," *Studies in American Jewish Literature* 5 (1986) 119-28.

Cuddihy, John Murray. "Jews, Blacks and the Cold War at the Top." *Worldview* 15: 2 (1972) 30-40.

Daniels, Sally "Recent Fiction: Flights and Evasions," *Minnesota Review* 2 (1962) 546-57.

DeMott, Benjamin. "Jewish Writers in America: A Place in the Establishment," *Commentary* 31 (1961) 31-43.

Dickstein, Morris. "Cold War Blues: Notes on the Culture of the Fifties," *Partisan Review* 41: 1 (1964) 30-53.

Dilsky, John. "Roth, Updike, and the High Expense of Spirit," *University of Windsor Review* 5: 1 (1969) 71-85.

Federman, Raymond. "Displaced Person: The Jew/The Wanderer/The Writer," *Denver Quarterly* 19: 1 (1984) 85-100.

Feuer, Lewis. "From Pluralism to Multiculturalism," *Society* (1991) 6-11.

Fiedler, Leslie A. "In the Interest of Surprises and Delight," *Folio* 20 (1955) 17-20.

_____. "The Commonplace as Absurd," *Reconstructionist* 24 (1958) 22-24.

Field, Leslie. "A Day in the life of Charlie Dubin's Son," *Studies in American Jewish Literature* 7: 2 (1988) 213-23

Finemna, Irving. "The Image of the Jew in our Fiction," *Tradition* 9 (1966) 19-47.

Freese, Peter. "Exploring the Post-Apocalypse: Bernard Malamud's *God's Grace*," *American Studies* 32: 4 (1987) 407-30.

Friedman, Allen Warren. "Bernard Malamud: The Hero as Schnook," *Southern Review* 4 (1968) 927-44.

_____. "The Jew's Complaint in Recent American Fiction: Beyond Exodus and Still in the Wilderness," *Southern Review* 8 (1972) 41-59.

Geismar, Maxwell. "The Jewish Heritage in Contemporary American Fiction," *Ramparts* 2 (1963) 5-13.

Gellen, Jozsef. "Ethnic Criticism and Ethnicity in American Literature," *John O'Hara Journal* 5: 1-2 (1983) 90-96.

Geyer, Michael. "Multiculturalism and the Politics of General Education," *Critical Inquiry* (1993) 17-23.

Glazar, Nathan. "In Defense of Multiculturalism," *New Republic* (1991) 102-15.

Glicksberg, Charles I. "The Literature of Absurdity," *Western Humanities Review* 12: 1 (1958) 29-37.

Greenberg, Alving. "A Sense of Place in Modern Fiction: The Novelist's World and the Allegorist's Heaven," *Genre* 5 (1972) 353-66.

_____. "Paradoxical Impossibility in Contemporary Fiction," *Contemporary Literature* 7: 1 (1966) 103-24.

Guttmann, Allen. "Out of the Ghetto and on to the Field: Jewish Writers and the Theme of Sports," *American Jewish History* (March 1985) 274-86

Harper, Howard M. Jr. "Trends in Recent American Fiction," *Contemporary Literature* 12 (1971) 204-29.

Harrison, Walter L. "Six Pointed Diamond: Baseball and American Jews," *Journal of Popular Culture* 15: 3 (1981) 112-18.

Hassan, Ihab. "Quest for the Subject: The Self in Literature," *Contemporary Literature* 29: 3 (1988) 420-37.

_____. "The Way Down and Out: Spiritual Deflection in Recent American Fiction," *Virginia Quarterly Review* 39: 1 (1963) 81-93.

Hertz, Robert N. "Quest for Identity: Jews and the American Dream," *The Midwest Quarterly* 5: 3 (1964) 231-48.

Howe, Irving. "Mass Society and Post-Modern Fiction," *Partisan Review* 24 (1959) 420-36.

Kauvar, Elaine M. "Introduction: Some Reflections on Contemporary American Jewish Culture," *Contemporary Literature* 34: 3 (1993) 337-58.

Kay, Helen. "*God's Grace*: The Language of Art or Polemics?," *MELUS* 13: 3-4 (1986) 49-54.

Kellman, Steven G. "Jews, Beasts, and American," *Studies in American Jewish Literature* 5 (1986) 61-68.

Kulik, Gary. "Special Issue on Multiculturalism: Editor's Introduction," *American Quarterly* (1993) 11-19.

Lewis, Stuart A. "The Jewish Author Looks at the Black," *Colorado Quarterly* 21: 3 (1973) 317-30

Matsutori, Mataki, "An Introduction to American Jewish Literature," *Western Humanities Review* 16 (1975) 34-49.

Mayfr, William H. Jr. "Jewish Literature in America: Impossible Assimilation under the 'Tyrannous Eye,'" *Western Humanities Review* 38: 4 (1984) 303-13.

Nilsen, Helge Normann. "Trends in Jewish-American Prose: A Short Historical Survey," *English Studies* 64: 6 (1983) 507-17.

Parks, John G. "The Terrors of Freedom: Religious Crisis in Recent American Fiction," *Northwest Review* 67: 2 (1982) 182-91.

Pifer, Ellen. "Malamud's Unnatural *The Natural*," *Studies in American Jewish Literature* 7: 2 (1988) 132-51.

Poger, Sidney. "American Jewish Fiction: Local Color Movement of the Fifties," *CLA Journal* 10: 3 (1975) 404-41.

Raffel, Burton. "Bernard Malamud," *The Literary Review* 13: 2 (1970) 149-55

Rorty, Ametie Oksenberg. "The Hidden Politics of Cultural Identification," *Political Theory* (1994) 104-15.

Tarcy, Robert. "A Sharing of Obsessions," *Southern Review* 6: 3 (1970) 890-94.

Weber, Daniel B. "Society and the American Novel, 1920-1960," *American Studies in Philippiness* 2: 1 (1966) 3-14.

Walden, Daniel. "A Mosaic of Jewish Writers: An Introduction," *Studies in American Jewish Literature* 2 (1982) 1-10.

______. "Bernard Malamud, An American Jewish Writer and His Universal Heroes," *Studies in American Jewish Literature* 7.2 (1988) 153-61.

Walzer, Michael. "Multiculturalism and Individualism," *Dissent* (1994) 8-18.

Winthrop, Henry. "The Alienation of Post-Industrial Man." *The Midwest Quarterly* 9: 2 (1968) 121-37.

Williams, Walter E. "Race, Scholarship, and Affirmative Action," *National Review* (1989) 21-27.

Witherington, Paul. "Malamud's Allusive Design in *A New Life*," *Western American Literature* 10 (1975) 115-23.

Woolf, Michael P. "The Madman as Hero in Contemporary American Fiction," *Journal of American Studies* 10: 2 (1976) 257-69.

# Index